The H

by John Krizanc

with an afterword by
Richard Paul Knowles

First published in 1990 by
House of Anansi Press Limited
34 Lesmill Rd.
Toronto, Canada
M3B 2T6

ISBN 0-88784-501-0

For production rights contact: Patricia Ney, Christopher Banks & Associates Inc., 219 Dufferin St., Ste. 305,Toronto, Ontario M6K 1Y9

The playwright and publisher gratefully acknowledge authorization to reprint
"Everybody Knows"
(Sharon Robinson, Leonard Cohen)
1988 HB Music Corp., Geffen Music,
Robinhill Music & Stranger Music, Inc.
All rights reserved. Used by permission.

The Half of It was first produced in Toronto by the Necessary Angel Theatre Company in association with Canadian Stage at The Stage Downstairs, with the following cast:

Kilman/Newman–John Bourgeois; Hillary–Lisa Bunting; Peter–Greg Ellwand; Jillson–Nick Guadagni; Dee–Janet Land; Clare–Sheila Moore; Frederick–Gordon Pinsent; Director–Richard Rose; Assistant Director–Rod Carley; Dramaturge–Don Kugler; Set and Lights Design–Graeme Thomson; Design Assistant–John Cuthbertson; Costume Design–Charlotte Dean; Video Design–Chris Clifford; Sound Design–Richard Mendonca; Production Manager (NAT)–Terry Crack; Production Manager (CSC)–Kent McKay; Wardrobe–Sophie Martin; Props–Leslie Davidson; Stage Manager–Sarah Stanley; ASM–André Czernohorsky; General Manager–Jerry Doiron.

Printed in Canada

The world is a comedy to those that think,
a tragedy to those that feel.

HORACE WALPOLE

In the great drama of existence
we are simultaneously actors and spectators

NIELS BOHR

I believe that for the individual who sees narrow rationalism
as having lost its persuasive power and who does not either
consider the magic of a mystical attitude . . . to be effective
enough, nothing remains but to put oneself at the mercy of these
aggravated opposites and their conflicts in one way or another. It
is in just that way that the researcher, more or less consciously,
can tread an inner way to salvation. Internal images, phantasies,
or ideas then slowly evolve as compensation for the external
situation, and they show an approach of the poles of the pairs of
opposites is possible.

WOLFGANG PAULI

If a man walk in the woods for love of them half of each day,
he is in danger of being regarded as a loafer;
but if he spends his whole day as a speculator,
sharing off the woods and making earth bald before her time,
he is esteemed an industrious and enterprising citizen.

HENRY DAVID THOREAU

CHARACTERS

JILLSON ASHE   Age 32. An ex-science teacher.

HILLARY ASHE   Age 29-30. Jill's sister, a real-estate broker.

PETER MALCHUK   Age 34. Jill's boyfriend, manages an ecological investment fund.

FREDERICK (FREDDY) BOISE   Age 60. Stock market speculator/manipulator.

CLARE ASHE   Age 55, but looks 45. Jill's mother.

KILMAN/NEWMAN   As Kilman he is Boise's spy, as Newman he is Jill's lover. Age 35.

DEE   A "bimbo" secretary, a radical feminist embezzler, age 25-35.

There is also some doubling:

Magdelaina (the maid)	
A nurse	
An amputee, beggar	
Kate Riley	Passing images
A bag lady	no dialogue
A pregnant woman	

Jill's dead father, David Ashe, is doubled by various actors, though his lines are spoken offstage by the actor who plays Kilman.

Dee will have a few lines in Act II as a policewoman.

Kilman will have a couple of lines in Act II as a scuba diver.

ACT ONE

> Everybody knows that the dice are loaded
> Everybody rolls with their fingers crossed
> Everybody knows the war is over
> Everybody knows the goods guys lost
> Everybody knows the fight was fixed
> The poor stay poor and the rich get rich
>
> That's how it goes
> Everybody knows
>
> Everybody knows the boat is leaking
> Everybody knows the captain lied
> Everybody got this broken feeling
> Like their father or their dog just died
> Everybody talking to their pockets
> Everybody wants a box of chocolates
> And a long-stemmed rose
> Everybody knows—

The music goes from loud to full blast and then bangs off.
*Lights up slowly. The curtain is still closed, but in front of it stands
JILLSON ASHE, an interesting-looking woman in her early thirties
in a black dress. There is a blackboard behind her. On it are written
several phrases: "Mind/Body," "Nature vs. Reason," and "Dead or
Alive?" She is moving her lips, but we still can't hear what she's
saying until the lights are fully up.*

JILL
. . . and it wasn't once upon a time, but at a specific time
not so long ago, when we still looked upon the world and
saw everything in it as equal to ourselves, because every-

thing was alive. If we needed branches for our shelter we would ask the tree's forgiveness before cutting it down. And if a rock didn't move, it wasn't because it was dead but because it was sleeping. Occasionally we met bad spirits in the forest, but we always knew a good spirit we could call on to protect us.

Now, as individuals formed themselves into tribes it was inevitable that hierarchies should develop and that our view of nature should change to reflect this . . . that the tribal chief should make an offering to the chief of all deer spirits, whatever. Thousands of years pass and eventually all these spirits are reduced to one life force—God—and this is called . . . anyone? (*pause*) Monotheism.

Now, if this guy—and it's interesting that we usually think God is masculine and the earth is feminine—if this God is up there somewhere, the life force is up there somewhere, then the earth is dead. It's no longer a source of magic and wonderment. We no longer have to thank the tree for its branch because we have it from God, the God that *we* invented, that all this stuff, this nature stuff, is here for the taking. This was, like—the biggest real-estate deal in history—the whole world. And the great thing about it was that it made it okay to cut down all the trees because really—they were dead already. You didn't have to feel guilty now, unlike before, when the earth was your mother. You never would have done such nasty things to your mother, would you? I heard that, Becky. . .

Anyway, we got this thing from God—the whole earth—it's a present from God. So, remember when you were a kid—what's the first thing you do with a present? (*points*) Ann? Play with it—a good answer. Unfortunately it may be the reason girls are discouraged by science. Do you have a brother? What would he do with his present? Find out how it works. How? Take it apart? Right. Now, when it comes to the world, the system that was developed for this purpose was called science.

Science was supposed to reveal the mysteries of creation and thereby bring us closer to God. Unfortunately He or She didn't want anything to do with us . . . maybe it was our breath? The trouble began when it became apparent to the scientists that what they were finding didn't jive with what the church was telling them they were supposed to find. This hurt their pride. They started to have doubts. They started thinking their own senses were deceiving them. Had God pulled the old cosmic wool over their eyes?

Determined to get to the bottom of all this, a fun guy named Francis Bacon suggested scientists should tie nature to the rack and torture her secrets from her. . . . The boys started playing for keeps. They wanted to find the truth, a truth which was experimentally verifiable and quantifiable, a one-plus-one-always-equals-two kind of truth. You'll notice I said the truth, because for most scientists how something works is equal to its truth.

In what became traditional science you and I are reduced to nothing but valves and pumps. Yet surely we have a uniqueness beyond the mechanisms which give us life.

This term, we'll delve into that question by exploring some of the ways in which recent science has realized the limitations of traditional reductionism.

Kimberly? (*beat*) No. I said at the beginning none of this is in your textbook. Like it or not, our knowledge is always evolving, and since science has come to be the way through which we interpret the world, it's important that we keep up with new developments, or else the way we see the world will be a little out of focus.

A concept like the survival of the fittest may have been indispensable for the success of the industrial revolution, but you only have to breathe the air to know it's been devastating for the environment. And yet it's an idea which has gone from fact to myth, and been bastardized into clichés like "dog eat dog," and no one ever stops to say, "I've never seen a dog eat a dog!" Corky? . . . Absolutely. There are lots of predators—but they wouldn't survive if they ate all their prey. Nor will we if we use up all nature's resources. The point is balance—it's moving away from the idea of self-interest to mutual interest. Nature is filled with co-operation and harmony, yet we prefer not to see it. We prefer to see only what allows us to justify our own self-interest.

Even your parents' decision to send you here to Grace can be seen as a Darwinian attempt to consolidate advantage by keeping you out of touch with an inferior gene pool. My parents certainly saw it like that.

By the way, if you hate the place as much as I did, just tell your mother you're thinking of becoming a lesbian.

Now, where was—(*a school bell rings*) Okay, tomorrow we'll start to look at the collapse of objectivity in contemporary physics. (*sound of students closing books, she has to talk over the noise*) Ann? (*points to student*) Right. Homework. When you go home I want you to ask your parents . . . "What is reality, and how much does it cost?"

BLACKOUT.

The curtain comes up to reveal a grassy hillside. There is a pond (a real pond) in the foreground. In this country setting we find a modern desk, a bed, and a Louis XIV loveseat. They define, with the pond, the four main playing areas. All the flats are painted, some with trees, some sky. The dominant image should be nature and there should be as many hidden entrances as possible.

SCENE 2

JILL's bedroom.

JILL enters in her black dress, holding an elegant dress to her body. Her sister, HILLARY, is wearing a check-and-stripe suit which somehow still manages to convey a certain stylishness. She pours two drinks.

JILL

But is it me?

HILLARY

It's certainly a change. Unemployment obviously suits you. Now me, if I didn't have a job I wouldn't have a personality.

JILL

I don't know that I can trust my own opinion anymore. I thought I was doing a good job teaching.

HILLARY

And you probably were, but parents don't want their kids challenged, they want them reinforced.

JILL

They're not concrete.

HILLARY

Always—up against it—always pushing it.

JILL

(*as she takes off the black dress*) I'm tired of being like that—tired of being outside. Peter . . . I don't know how he does it, but he's not upset by the world. He's somehow able to keep his integrity and still be optimistic.

HILLARY

Hopefully it will rub off.

JILL

When I'm with him it's real . . . comfy.

HILLARY

Jill, comfy starts at half a million.

JILL

Well, I love his brand of . . . normalcy.

HILLARY

Maybe he's normal to you, but to Mom he'll just be . . . Polish. Her idea of a normal guy is some blue-blood whose piss is naturally carbonated.

JILL

Normal's the wrong word. (*takes a drink*) Actually, it's more like he's noble.

HILLARY

Noble's all right. Noble does the dishes. Me, I go for assertive. Assertive has a maid.

JILL

Hills, I'd like your opinion about him.

HILLARY

Are you going to let me see you in that dress or not? Because I should go.

JILL

(*putting on the dress and talking from under it*) What do you think?

HILLARY

Honestly, I think he's great. He's an environmentalist with an ambition—the perfect balance—try it.

JILL

(*offering her black dress*) Peter says I've got too much black. Are you sure you don't want this?

HILLARY

I told you, Ronji absolutely forbids me to wear black. It collapses my aura.

JILL

What's that—like a collapsed lung?

HILLARY

(*lighting a cigarette*) Business is up. Listen, when you're selling 4,000 square-foot houses you've got to fill them with "buy" feelings. That's what this outfit does for me. It helps me expand my aura until it fills the whole house.

JILL

Where do people put their furniture?

HILLARY

Now, what this needs is a few accessories—and Jill, hair under the arms isn't one of them. (*takes off her scarf and her printed handbag and puts them on JILL*)

JILL

How do you do it, Hills? How come things are so easy for you?

HILLARY

You've got to learn to mix and match. A little Buddha, little New Age, touch of Jew. Mix and match. A few years ago I'd have died before wearing checks and stripes—now it works for me. And I don't clash with the world. (*looking at her watch*) Shit. I've got to run. I'm late for Chinese.

JILL

You're studying Chinese?

HILLARY

(*downing her drink*) Yeah, well, they're my biggest clients—and I've got a gorgeous tutor.

JILL

Say something.

HILLARY

Ni you hen pyaulyanjde naitou. (*phonetics: Ni yo han pyauliangda naito*)

JILL

What's it mean?

HILLARY

You have lovely nipples. (*pause*) It'll work out. Bye. (*takes her purse off JILL, gives her a quick kiss and exits*)

SCENE 3

PETER mysteriously pops out of the empty bed and immediately hurls a pillow at JILL and starts whacking her with his pillow. She hits back aggressively—feathers fly—they fall onto the bed laughing.

PETER

Feel better?

JILL

(*hits him again*) Yes.

PETER

(*as he undoes her dress*) Now you're going to let go of all that regret and frustration. You quit your job. It's over.

JILL

But was it the right thing to do?

PETER

Jill—your own students complained about you. Your own students.

JILL

Well, they're their parents' children, aren't they?

PETER

Exactly. And to get them round to some other way of looking at things—you've got to do it gradually. Sell the benefits.

JILL

(*kisses him*) Seduce them?

PETER

(*taking off her dress*) Find the common ground—

JILL

We're all mammals—

PETER

You're so eloquent about co-operation and empathy and yet you attack the very people you're trying to change.

JILL

(*playfully, with her hands clasped in prayer*) Forgive me, Father Peter, I lack your ecclesiastical patience. I get so frustrated.

PETER

My child (*sings like a Gregorian chant*), I can heal your frustration, but intercourse demands a middle ground.

(*stroking the inside of her thighs*) There is a lot of possibilities in the middle ground.

JILL

(*falling back on her elbows*) I'm beginning to feel them.

PETER

Then open yourself to them. . . . It could be that you won't end up teaching at all.

JILL

What then?

PETER

When I was . . . well, anyway, before my parents died, I thought all I could do was work in a coal mine like my father—(*slips his hand under her slip and removes her panties*) And look where I ended up.

JILL

Pretty close to where you began. (*sits up suddenly, curious*) Do you realize you always skip over their deaths?

PETER

(*kissing her*) No, I don't.

JILL

Sometimes you mention the fire, but it's as if your life begins at seventeen.

PETER

(*having lost the moment*) It's just that when I try to remember . . . I can picture the house before the fire, but when I go inside . . . there's nothing there.

JILL

Literally?

PETER

If I strain, I can hear Dad coughing or Mom saying it's all right I failed grade nine, "just as long as you did your best."

JILL

You wouldn't fail in my class.

PETER

But was it me? I don't feel like I'm remembering my own life. That life belonged to someone else and for all I know he's working in the coal mines.

JILL

(*animated*) It may turn out that you're working in a real mine. There's a theory, derived from quantum physics, which says that all possible universes exist. In other words, in one universe you died in the fire, in another your parents survived. Universes could be constantly emerging, branching out, and running parallel to each other with every possibility.

PETER

Then in some universe you're still teaching school, you never quit your job?

JILL

I wish.

The lights pop up in the ASHES' living room. A painted flat is opened, like a double door, by the ASHES' maid, Magdelaina. As she exits, DAVID ASHE appears. He is dressed for a costume ball as a French aristocrat of the 16th century. He wears a period wig and a distinctive mask. He flips a coin. His wife, CLARE, is also dressed in costume, looking like Marie-Antoinette. She talks to her daughter HILLARY in the foyer.

CLARE

Quitting in mid-term. Have you heard what your daughter Jillson's done, David? I always said Jillson has a complete inability to finish things. She was born six weeks premature and she's been leaving early ever since.

DAVID ASHE picks up a telephone.
JILL picks up the phone by the bed just as DAVID ASHE clutches his chest and falls over. The lights in the ASHE's living room go black. This is the first of many images JILL will see. There should be a special light and perhaps a sound cue to distinguish them from "reality."

JILL

Hello? (*pause*) Didn't it ring?

PETER

No.

JILL

(*puts down the phone*) I haven't told Mom I quit.

PETER

I thought you did that weeks ago.

JILL

I just told Dad.

PETER

And they don't talk?

JILL

He wanted me to explain it.

PETER

C'mon, you quit your job. It's not as if you quit the Book-of-the-Month Club. (*hands her the phone*) Call her.

JILL

Now?

PETER

Tell her she's ruining my sex life.

JILL

(*dials*) She was against my teaching, so this will be a victory for her.

PETER

Jill—

JILL

What?

PETER

The middle ground—

JILL

(*nods yes*) It's busy. (*puts the phone down*)

JILL kisses PETER as the lights fade to black.

SCENE 4

FREDDY BOISE crashes through a wall to enter his office. He talks on an "earphone."

BOISE

Angel, don't talk to me about fundamentals. . . . This is a stock, for Christ's sake, perception is value—keep shorting it—down, Angel, down. (*pause*) Because when it hits twenty the institutions will puke it up with lunch.

Enter KILMAN. As he crosses, the lights come up and we see DAVID in costume, sitting on the bed beside his daughter JILLSON. PETER sleeps beside her.

BOISE

(*with hand over mouthpiece*) What?

KILMAN

(*crossing to him*) The Life Products board is having an emergency meeting. They're voting now. (*listens intently on his headphone*)

BOISE

(*into phone*) Hold on. (*to KILMAN*) And?

DAVID kisses JILL goodbye and departs.

JILL

(*bolting up*) Dad? Daddy!

JILL jumps up and begins to dress. PETER gets up, yawns, and heads out. BOISE and KILMAN continue to talk over this action.

KILMAN

They've decided to announce a dividend reduction on Monday.

BOISE

How much?

KILMAN

Five cents instead of twenty. (*"high-fives" BOISE*)

BOISE

Angel—they're cutting dividends—fifteen cents — Monday. Happy? So, fuck it into the ground and put a stake through its heart. Right. Once you break twenty I'll start accumulating. (*pause*) That's not necrophilia, Angel. Necrophilia is when you still lust after your wife. (*hangs up*) Anything else?

KILMAN

That other matter—I found her. (*hands BOISE a file*)

BOISE

(*after opening the file*) That will be all, Kilman.

BOISE reads the file with interest as his office fades to black. KILMAN walks across the stage, passing JILL. As he does, an oxygen tent flies down. The mask of DAVID ASHE in a hospital gown inside the tent, tells us where we are. We hear the sound of a heart monitor . . . and after a time we hear an axe cutting down a tree.

SCENE 5

JILL is sitting on the side of her father's hospital bed.

JILL

(*zips open the oxygen tent to hold her father's hand. Remembering*) Daddy, you're crying—

DAVID's voice is done by the actor who's playing KILMAN. All DAVID's dialogue is voice-over; we hear it over speakers.

DAVID

Hello, chipmunk. You found me. Is the party over?

JILL

You were crying.

DAVID

So, you're ten years old. A bloody decade. Who'd have thought? Happy birthday, Jilly.

The chopping stops. The lights come up off to one side on an old wooden wheelbarrow which contains compost, a shovel, and a Russian olive tree. We notice a small tree stump nearby.

JILL

A Russian olive—

DAVID

Happy Birthday.

JILL

How come it's not a willow? All along the banks, there's willow. We always plant willows on special occasions.

DAVID

It's time for a change. Don't you like it?

JILL

I love it. What happened to this one? Why'd you cut it down?

DAVID

It's dead. Now I've got a spot for yours on the other side.

JILL

Did you plant this one, Dad?

A NURSE enters and zips up the oxygen tent.

DAVID

. . . first one I ever planted.

JILL

Who for?

DAVID

A little girl. A little girl who drowned.

The nurse holds up the bed sheet. JILL helps and peers inside. The NURSE removes a catheter bag full of urine and exits.

JILL

How? When, Dad?

DAVID

We were both around ten. We were up here in the winter and decided to run away. Kate . . . Kate Riley insisted on going across the pond—I said the ice wasn't thick enough. I did, but she insisted. There was a loud cracking sound. . . . I turned and she was gone. . . . Enough about it.

JILL

Did the crocodiles get her?

DAVID

She just disappeared. When spring came I planted this willow and now it's gone and died too.

JILL

Shh—there's Mom. Hide.

Long pause. The heart monitor continues throughout.

SCENE 6

JILL is with her father as CLARE bursts in.

CLARE

Ah, David—Jillson?

JILL

Hello, Mother. (*gives her a kiss*)

CLARE

I love you too, dear. (*breaking away*) I've brought you some tulips, David. There's a young man at the soup kitchen keeps bringing me presents. I expect he stole these from the park across the road. Still, it's the thought. (*puts the flowers in a vase on the end-table beside her settee*)

JILL

I don't think he's going to wake up.

CLARE

He's just resting—aren't you, David? You just need a long sleep, like last time. (*to JILL*) Remember last time? He woke up after three days with twice the energy. God, I could use a rest—here all night. Then the opera committee this morning, and the soup kitchen at lunch. We're short-staffed again.

JILL

I . . . I've some time. I could help out.

CLARE

You? Jill, this is the Junior League. You hate Junior League.

JILL

If it would help you.

CLARE

Don't think you can make headway with me. I shouldn't even be speaking to you.

JILL

You've heard?

CLARE

We were just heading out to the Thompsons' costume ball. David insisted on dressing as Henri the third. I told him I was going to be Marie-Antoinette, but would he be Louis? Honestly. Who is Henri the third? He looked like a rabbi. And then Hillary dropped in. The shock of it.

JILL

Now it's my fault?

CLARE

Fired from Grace School. Fired.

JILL

I quit.

CLARE

Don't be "moot" with me. It seems that when you weren't advocating lesbianism—

JILL

I was joking—

CLARE

(*rolling on*) You had all the girls worshipping trees, trying to turn them into Druids. Is that true?

JILL

No, Mother.

CLARE

Of course it's true.

JILL

I was trying to teach them that how we view the world is culturally conditioned. It was a preamble to introducing them to quantum mechanics.

CLARE

People don't send their girls to private school to meet mechanics. (*smiles*) Really, Jill. I was against this teaching business from the start, but your father . . . you've spent altogether too much time looking through microscopes and staring at the stars to see the real world. I don't know why you can't learn from your sister.

JILL

I'm trying.

CLARE

She's doing ever so well in real estate and she's met a junior partner—

JILL

—at Tory and Tory—

CLARE

—and that was the other point I wanted to raise. This Peter—

JILL

Yes, Mother . . . he is Polish.

CLARE

Do I know the family?

JILL

Not in *Who's Who*.

CLARE

Really, Jill, I'm as progressive as the next. I'm just curious. Catholic?

JILL

Yes.

CLARE

Thank God your grandmother's not here. Still, I suppose a little company is a good thing.

JILL

(*kisses her father goodbye*) Peter's moved in with me, Mother.

CLARE

Moved in?

JILL

We were going to get a new place, but they're all too expensive.

CLARE

Moved in?

JILL

Yes. Bye. (*exits*)

CLARE

(*after a beat, to her husband*) David, you're the only person I know who can glare at me with his eyes closed. I was going to say I was happy for her. I was, but as usual she had to leave in time to think the worst of me.

CLARE sits with her husband. The lights stay up. The heart monitor continues.

SCENE 7

In BOISE's office. BOISE has opened a cupboard door to reveal a video monitor. KILMAN enters as BOISE watches a video tape on a monitor which shows PETER moving in to JILL's apartment in a small rundown Victorian house. A dishevelled legless woman who propels herself along on a four-wheeled board stops and puts out her hand for money. PETER awkwardly reaches into his pocket to give her a bill.

BOISE

(*talking over the video*) He's the one?

KILMAN

They've been together for about six weeks now.

BOISE

Together . . . how?

KILMAN

Aside from mornings at his office and his time at the university, they're together all the time. As you can see, he's moved in.

BOISE

You said they were dating, for Christ's sake.

KILMAN

It didn't seem serious . . . maybe it's to save money.

BOISE

When a man wants to save money, he generally leaves the woman. (*looking at the tape, now at the part where PETER is giving money to the bag lady*) He gave that thing five dollars! Five dollars!

KILMAN

Yes, well, this fund of his only has 900,000 under management, and then he just makes 15,000 a year as a teaching assistant.

BOISE

Teaching what?

KILMAN

Ecological investing.

BOISE

Is he any good?

KILMAN

(*nods yes*) In an ethical sort of way.

BOISE

So he's poor?

KILMAN

Yes. And it doesn't appear as if Jill takes anything from her family.

BOISE

Getting personal.

KILMAN

Sir?

BOISE

"Jill."

KILMAN

"Miss Ashe," then.

BOISE

I presume the place is wired?

KILMAN

There's a bug on the phone beside the bed, picks up everything within forty feet, so we hear pretty near everything. Just push this button and you'll hear it live.

KILMAN pushes the button and the lights pop up on JILL. PETER is off dressing and JILL is changing for the funeral. CLARE is still at DAVID's bedside.

JILL

It was like he was just sunbathing. "Just resting," she said. She couldn't see he was dying.

PETER

(*off*) She can't be that bad.

JILL

Wait till you meet her. She has this kind of fascist enthusiasm. It's like watching Charles Manson play Gidget . . . and I stood there as dumb as a beachball.

In DAVID ASHE's hospital room a buzzer from a heart monitor sounds. CLARE runs out calling "Nurse! Nurse!" The oxygen tent flies up to the ceiling.

PETER

(*enters putting on his shirt and tie*) Are you sure you're being fair? Look what she's going through. She probably wasn't thinking.

JILL

She's always thinking, that's her problem. That's the problem with all of us. A world full of "decent-thinking" people and look at it. If only we would feel a little more.

PETER

Go back to swinging in trees, is that it? (*goes off*)

JILL

At least animals aren't going to destroy the planet. Lake trout aren't going to jump out of the water and push the button. Maybe there'd be peace if the President was some great big cuddly orangutan who sat around all day eating mangoes and masturbating—

PETER and KILMAN laugh at this.

PETER

(*re-entering*) From your mother to masturbation. (*puts on his pants*)

JILL

But they are related. The reason I'm so frustrated by her is that she's frozen every emotion.

PETER

Come on.

JILL

If you don't express things, they go bad.

PETER

Yes, but you're the one with these feelings, you're the one who isn't saying what you feel. You can't presume to know her intimate thoughts. Deal with yours, it might help to change hers. Are these pants all right?

BOISE abruptly switches the conversation off as the lights fade to black in PETER and JILL's space.

BOISE

No wonder she can't get a job.

KILMAN

Well, I've been listening to her all week, and I think she makes a strange kind of . . . (*catching BOISE looking at him*) Anyway, they talk like that for hours. And then they . . .

BOISE

What?

KILMAN

Well, they talk a lot—

BOISE

(*understanding*) That's enough.

The lights go to black on BOISE's space.

SCENE 8

CLARE ASHE has already appeared in the foyer of her living room. She is dressed in black. She stares out a window frame with her back to the audience; she is lit by a surreal light. Meanwhile, JILL is in her room and still talking to PETER, who is offstage.

JILL

It's terrible, but sometimes I imagine she's not my mother at all. . . . And then I get mad at myself—mad for being angry. I want to share in her grief. Why won't she let me . . . hold her?

JILL goes over to her mother and acts out what she says.

JILL

. . . rock her . . . say, we'll survive . . . I love you . . . I'm here . . . or not have to say anything.

CLARE ASHE turns around just as PETER enters, adjusting his tie.

The light on CLARE is suddenly normal.

JILL

(*offering an arm*) Mom, we should leave.

CLARE

(*ignoring Jill*) So you're Peter.

PETER

I'd hoped we'd meet under more—

CLARE

Not a word. Take my arm, Peter. I need a strong arm now. Shall we go?

They exit upstage as we hear funeral organ music. BOISE appears unseen by all and holds open the door of the crematorium as PETER exits the other door. He wipes away a tear.

SCENE 9

Outside the crematorium. PETER enters to encounter BOISE.

BOISE

Shouldn't you be with Jill?

PETER

The service is over. I didn't want to see the cremation. The flames . . .

BOISE

(*lights a cigar*) You don't actually see them.

PETER

No?

BOISE

No. Everything's done behind closed doors. We never see the important things, do we?

PETER

Did you know him?

BOISE

Yes. Long time ago. Things come to a conclusion — resolve — his death was a small part of that resolution.

PETER

I don't—

BOISE

It was another life.

PETER

Jill talked about him, but unfortunately I never got to meet him.

BOISE

I suppose you can learn a lot about a girl from meeting her father.

PETER

Always imagined I'd be asking him for his permission to marry her.

BOISE

Is that still done?

PETER

They're a very traditional family.

BOISE

True. Well, you've got a good jaw. They're big on bone

structure, as I remember. Too bad about the last name. Malchuk. Ukrainian, is it?

PETER

Polish.

BOISE

Ah. I'm sure you'll find Clare very progressive. Anyway, it really is Jill's decision. Only Jill's. Clare may not spring for the terrace at the yacht club, but she'll go along with Jill. Have you asked?

PETER

No. I wanted to be a bit more established in my business before—we haven't actually met, have we?

Organ music begins to play in the chapel.

BOISE

It's over, Peter.

PETER

I should go back.

BOISE

Yes.

PETER exits into the chapel. BOISE exits in the opposite direction.

PETER

How did you know my . . . (*enters the chapel*)

A procession exits the crematorium. CLARE carries DAVID's ashes in an urn. JILL follows with HILLARY. In the background we hear organ music.
As the others exit off, JILL sees a veiled and pregnant bride carrying an urn. Jill turns and lifts the bride's veil so that only she can see her face. The bride gives her the urn.

BLACKOUT.

SCENE 10

Night. JILL sits by the edge of the pond. As PETER's flashlight, the sole source of light, comes on, we see that JILL is putting her father's ashes in the pond. We hear the sound of crickets.

JILL

You'd think it would just be ash, yet there's all these bits of bone.

PETER

Never saw my parents after the fire—they said there was nothing left.

JILL

(*reaching out for his leg*) I'm sorry, Peter. I didn't mean to . . .

PETER

Can I?

JILL gives him a small bone fragment.

I wonder if there's always some part of us, some small bit of finger which hangs on to the world. (*pause. Drops the fragment into the water. Stares at the water*) We should—(*goes to exit*)

JILL

Not yet. I've never seen the pond like this—choppy . . . hungry.

PETER

It's really more like a lake, isn't it?

As PETER is saying this, he pans the audience with his thin-beamed flashlight.

JILL

I suppose. (*tosses a small bone fragment in the water*)

PETER

What's that? With the rusty fence?

JILL

Tennis court.

PETER

And that? (*pans and the light reveals a large, frightening crocodile beside the small stump of the willow DAVID planted for KATHLEEN RILEY. Pause*) Jill?

JILL

What?

JILL stares at the crocodile, which PETER cannot see.

PETER

That paved area, by the willows?

JILL

Oh, that's the shuffleboard. I liked shuffleboard because they didn't make me wear my whites.

PETER takes the light off the crocodile—we do not see it again. The frogs and crickets resume.

PETER

Did you and Hillary just play games all day?

JILL

Hills was hardly here. She spent most summers at tennis camp or sailing school. Anything to get away from one of Dad's history lessons. He could sit you down beside an old oak stump and go through each ring—over 200 years of family history. Hillary's idea of history is last month's *Vogue*.

PETER

So, you had a thousand acres to yourself?

JILL

There's a lot of wildlife. And being alone in the woods isn't like being alone in the city. There's a rightness to this place—the scale, the rhythm. From here, the trees look as thick as a wall. But it's a wall I can walk through. There's a stream down there, leads—still don't know where it leads, but I had a favourite spot in the woods. Dad was the only one who knew how to find me. It was a game, really—to give him an excuse to get away from Mom.

PETER

She's not as bad as that. She seemed—well, she's a bit imposing, intimidating.

JILL

(*after filling the urn with water from the pond, she now pours it out*) You know, when Dad was drunk he used to piss in the pond.

They laugh. PETER takes off his jacket, puts it over her shoulders, and sits down.

JILL

That's the only time he was ever spontaneous or when we went into the woods. But when he was in public, he was so mannered. Mum and him had these very public forms of address, always kissing and saying, "I love you, darling." I remember watching how their bodies stiffened when they kissed and thinking, it's not true. It's just not true.

PETER

Maybe after thirty years of marriage—

JILL

No, I'm talking about when I was four, five. I couldn't figure it out, because occasionally there were times with my father, picking strawberries, planting a tree, when he'd suddenly materialize in front of me, a real human being. And I'd think "here's the dad I love." Then we'd be walking back to the house and I'd turn to him and find myself holding hands with a stranger.

PETER

Which one was real?

JILL

Growing up in our family was like that famous paradox, where someone draws a square and writes in it, "Everything in this square is untrue."

PETER

The Liar's Paradox.

JILL

That was my family. If everything is untrue, then the statement's untrue, so everything must be true.

PETER

You're a fun date. (*hugs her and laughs*)

JILL

Come on, I'll show you my old bedroom.

PETER

You didn't tell Clare we were coming up here— did you?

JILL

No.

PETER

And she, she doesn't know you put the ashes in the pond?

JILL

It was something I promised. It's done now.

They exit up the hill.

SCENE 11

BOISE takes off his coat, shirt, and tie.

BOISE

Kilman!

KILMAN

(*entering rapidly*) Sir?

BOISE

For the girl—what, what button?

KILMAN

(*going over to the desk, which presumably has some terminal with a keyboard embedded in it*) Thirty-two, sir. (*pushes the button*)

At the same time HILLARY and CLARE have come down the hill to join JILL in her bedroom. An old window frame has appeared about five feet in front of JILL's bed.

HILLARY appears more casual than before. CLARE, in slacks, still manages to convey the classic elegance of Chanel or Valentino.

JILL

We could sit in the living room, Mother.

CLARE

I want to keep an eye on my car, dear. (*peers out the window*)

KILMAN

You're in luck.

JILL

It's safe.

BOISE

Get Dee in here, will you?

KILMAN goes to leave, then lingers, eager to hear.

CLARE

(*looking out the window*) Honestly, I had no idea you lived in such an environment.

HILLARY

Actually, this is a very up-and-coming neighbourhood. I think she should buy here.

CLARE

How can my daughter live in an area where people look at trash cans as if they're window-shopping?

JILL

Mother, this is the real world—the one you're always talking about.

CLARE

I'm sick and tired of hearing poverty referred to as the real world. As if the poor were somehow more real than I. They do not own the patent on suffering.

JILL

Well, whoever is leasing it to them must be rich.

CLARE glares at JILL

JILL and HILLARY share a smile.

BOISE

(*motioning KILMAN to go*) Kilman—

KILMAN exits.

CLARE

Do you two have any idea of what I've been through?

JILL

Mom, we both understand how hard it's been and want to—

CLARE

Lawyers, accountants, stabbing into my bank balance. You know what they did to Mrs. Stratton on Cluny? They showed her the finances, she got up, phoned Betsy Weir to cancel tennis, and then ran naked through a plate-glass window.

HILLARY

What's this about? You've never mentioned money in your life—

CLARE

And now she pushes a shopping cart about and dresses like a lumberjack.

JILL sees this Mrs. Stratton materialize, slowly pushing her cart.

HILLARY

Are you saying there's some sort of problem with Daddy's estate?

CLARE

Some sort of—there isn't an estate.

JILL

But Father had his life insurance, the house was paid for years—

CLARE

He gave most of it away. (*hands the woman a cake. The woman nibbles at it with her fingers*)

HILLARY

How much is left, Mother?

CLARE

It's so confusing. There's some bonds—

MRS. STRATTON exits.

HILLARY

How much?

CLARE

Treasury bills—

HILLARY

How much?

CLARE

I sold the stock—there's a black person beside my car.

JILL

(*looking out*) My landlord. That's his Mercedes across the street.

HILLARY

Jillson! Christ, Mother, how much is there?!

CLARE

Have we lost our manners too? . . . They say it amounts to a little over a million.

HILLARY

Plus the properties? The house in Lyford Cay should sell for—

CLARE

It was sold last year! Didn't tell me. He just sold it.

HILLARY

What about Burnham Wood? It ought be worth nine or ten million.

JILL

You're not serious?

CLARE

That's why I wanted to talk to both of you. Under the terms of your father's will, the three of us jointly own Burnham Wood.

HILLARY

(*happy*) Sell it!

JILL

We can't.

CLARE

Jillson, this isn't going to be easy, so please don't start on about how long it's been in the family.

JILL

Mom, you're not destitute. You own your own home and have a million in the bank.

HILLARY

It's our inheritance.

JILL

(*to HILLARY*) You made half a million last year. I'm sorry, I find it hard to sympathize.

KILMAN enters and whispers to BOISE that PETER is outside. BOISE nods.

HILLARY

Jill, with your share you can buy a place an hour north and still have money. In five years the woods will be surrounded by suburbs. There'll be a mall outside the gate. There'll be a Taco Bell—

JILL

(*quietly*) The woods aren't a resource, they're not money in the bank, and they don't just stand for a few hundred years of family history. Maybe Dad didn't know the value of money, but he understood the value of the woods.

HILLARY

It's just sitting there. It's a useless piece of land! Sell it—

JILL

It's their uselessness, their utter indifference to us, which gives the woods their value. They keep us humble—

HILLARY

Poverty keeps people humble.

HILLARY takes out a gun and shoots MRS. STRATTON, who was just about to re-enter. We hear the crash of her body and cart from the wings and see her feet sticking out from the curtain.

CLARE

(*acting as if nothing happened*) Those are nice sentiments, Jill, but you shouldn't presume to know your father's thoughts. I certainly never understood him.

BOISE notices KILMAN and indicates he should leave.

JILL

He asked me to scatter his ashes on the pond.

HILLARY

He didn't—

CLARE

Hillary . . . I knew about it.

HILLARY

Well, still . . . we can't afford to debate about what Daddy wanted. We have to sell.

CLARE

(*to JILL*) I'll ask the lawyers to see if they can't work something into the deed about "minimal development."

HILLARY

People don't buy if there's conditions.

CLARE

Jill?

PETER appears seemingly out of nowhere. Only JILL seems to notice him.

PETER

Jill—the middle ground.

JILL

Do what you're going to do.

JILL exits, pursued by CLARE and HILLARY.

CLARE

Jillson, don't you walk away. I'm trying to do what's right

for the whole family. Now I want you to say you understand.

PETER stands in place until KILMAN fetches him for his entrance in the next scene. DEE enters the office. BOISE is now lying on his desk with his shirt off. BOISE sees DEE and hits the off button. JILL's bedroom goes black. Her window frame flies up.

BOISE

Ready for your lesson?

DEE

Be gentle, or I'll walk on your back.

The next scene has begun.

SCENE 12

FREDDY BOISE lies on his desk. We notice that one of his arms is black up to the elbow. His buxom secretary DEE massages and oils his back. The two are looking at a computer screen embedded in the desk.

BOISE

Now, that column gives you the "market and size."

Enter KILMAN and PETER.

KILMAN

Peter Mal-shuk, sir. (*exits*)

PETER

Malchuk.

KILMAN exits.

BOISE

Welcome to my abattoir, Peter. Surprised to see me again?

PETER

I was more surprised when I realized our last talk was a job interview.

BOISE

Be right with you.

DEE

(*massaging his back, looks at the terminal*) Fifteen and a half to three-quarters, two by five. What's that mean?

BOISE

Somewhere out there some guy wants to buy two thousand shares at fifteen and a half and somebody else wants to sell five thousand at fifteen and three-quarters.

DEE

Do we buy?

BOISE

Peter?

PETER

What's the company?

BOISE

I haven't hired you yet.

The lights have slowly come up. We find CLARE reading in her chair. She reads by cutting a page out with an x-acto knife, holding it up, reading it, and letting it fall to the floor. She will read throughout the scene, unnoticed by all. Meanwhile, JILL is up at the woods, picking wildflowers.

PETER

If you're accumulating, I'd take it and see what's being offered at sixteen.

BOISE

Take it.

DEE

(*reaching out and pressing a few buttons on the terminal*)
It's two by ten. Do I buy?

BOISE

Wait.

DEE

Why?

PETER

Because the purpose of the exercise is to see if there's any competition for the stock.

BOISE

Precisely.

DEE

And if there isn't?

BOISE

Buy 9,000—never the whole lot—and just before the bell sell a few thousand so at the close it's down an eighth. Now, Peter—can I get you a drink?

PETER

No, thank you.

BOISE

(*sits up*) I understand you run a small fund which only invests in ecologically sound companies.

PETER

That's right. I've been charting about fifteen companies for the last five years.

BOISE

And the return?

PETER

Averages fifteen per cent.

BOISE

Hear that, Dee? Fifteen per cent. Not bad. Forgive me, I haven't introduced you. Peter Malchuk, this is Dee. She got an A in shiatsu at secretarial college.

DEE

Reflexology, actually.

PETER .

Hello. (*shakes her hand. Gets some lotion on it*)

DEE

Do you have trouble urinating?

PETER

Pardon? (*doesn't know what to do with the lotion on his hand. Failing to rub it in, he eventually wipes it on his hair*)

DEE

I can tell by the way you stand, it's the left heel. Prostate trouble, right?

PETER

(*shifting his stance*) There's nothing wrong with my bodily functions.

BOISE

Don't see why you're embarrassed, Peter. If Dee says there's something wrong with your pee, there must be. Excuse me.

BOISE exits briefly.

PETER

There isn't.

DEE

See how your heel's worn down? The imbalanced posture blocks the flow of energy. It all backs up, putting pressure on the prostate, which cuts off the urethra. Let me massage it.

PETER

Leave my . . . alone.

DEE

(*takes hold of Peter's foot*) Your heel. It's in your heel. Just below the left ankle. (*quickly removes his shoe and sock—leaving him standing on one foot*)

BOISE re-enters, his shirt open and his tie loose around his neck. He fixes two drinks from the bottle in JILL and PETER's room.

BOISE

As best as I can make out, your investment strategy is that there's money in goodness.

PETER

Ah . . . yes. I—I don't think the business, or the investment community at any rate, have caught on, that people, at least my generation, are willing to pay for environmentally safe products.

BOISE

Biodegradable diapers?

PETER

Sure, if there was such a thing. Three per cent of every landfill is made up of dirty diapers.

DEE

No shit?

PETER

Must you?

DEE

Three minutes—that's all.

BOISE

(*handing PETER a drink*) Here. I don't drink alone. Ah, you noticed the hand? Lost the real one in a motorcycle accident. Used to have a hook, but this new—do you know I personally sign all the cheques here? It can do it automatically. Just pull the thumb. Go on.

PETER hops over to the desk, dragging DEE, and pulls the thumb. BOISE, having already inserted a pen, demonstrates the hand by writing his name on a piece of paper.

PETER

(*impressed*) I read about it in an article in *Business Week.* They said it was also an electric toothbrush.

BOISE

(*pulls his pinky to stop the hand, but it doesn't stop*) It's the prosthetic equivalent of the Swiss Army knife. Glad to see you've done your homework. Then you know what they say about me.

PETER

I don't believe everything I read.

BOISE

And I didn't get to where I am by being good. If you're climbing a pole you can't stop to think about what's right, or the shoulds-and-should-nots start biting into you like fleas and tics. They paralyze you. (*by this point his hand moving about has become quite noticeable*) Goddamn hand. Why do you think they're always putting up statues to people with integrity? Because they're monuments to inaction. Liars are the real doers in this world, because we're blind to everything but up. (*points up*) Progress is that way, Peter.

DEE

(*to PETER*) Stand still.

PETER

You said you might be interested in investing. Frankly I'm not that hungry.

BOISE

I've been researching you too, Peter.

PETER

(*to DEE*) Please, can I have my foot?

BOISE

Let's be honest—

PETER

Don't change your habits on my account.

BOISE

I think your idea is . . . full of shit, Peter. But when Republicans start calling themselves environmentalists even I have to concede that all this talk about ecology might be more than just a passing fashion. (*still trying to stop his hand*)

PETER

It is. There's a new world emerging out there.

BOISE

And so . . . I'm prepared to invest fifteen million dollars, your way. I'll advance you a $50,000 management fee against your one per cent commission and I'll throw in an office down the hall.

PETER

There's at least ten other ecological funds which could—

BOISE

Whatta you got, a rainbow up your ass? I'm offering you a seat at the big table. Don't you want to create this new world? I'm offering you a chance to drop your drawers and fuck that world into existence.

PETER

I'm not interested in being some public relations window dressing while—Jesus! That hurt. (*he falls to the floor*)

BOISE

Am I pissing out a window here? Fifteen million is never window dressing. You say there's money to be made. I say do it. Prove it to me. Pick the companies—that's how things change—money runs after profit. Kilman!

DEE

Just let me do your bladder.

KILMAN bursts in.

BOISE

(*shaking his hand*) Get me the son-of-a-bitch who made this. (*bangs the hand on the edge of CLARE's loveseat, then points to his tie, which he has been unable to do up*) Do this, would ya?

KILMAN

(*does up the tie*) There's a problem. Someone's buying Life Products.

DEE

How much?

KILMAN

Thirty thousand. He's taking whatever's offered. It's at nineteen. I've got Angel on hold.

DEE

(*to PETER*) Stand still.

BOISE grabs the phone and dials, in what is usually CLARE ASHE's space.
The scene begins to race.

BOISE

Angel? Well, get him! (*bangs the arm down again and it finally stops*)

PETER

I can't do this for much longer.

KILMAN

Weren't you trying to buy some stock from that pension-fund manager over at Anstalt?

BOISE

They bought Life Products when it was trading at twenty-seven, 240,000 shares.

KILMAN

He wants lunch next week. (*watching PETER*)

DEE

(*to KILMAN*) It's his prostate.

PETER

Would you stop saying that?

BOISE

Angel, who's buying? Uh-huh. Hold. (*to KILMAN*)
Anstalt's broker is?

KILMAN

Usually Bunting.

BOISE

I'll take care of it, Angel. (*hangs up*) Bunting bought the
stock. How many shares have I got?

KILMAN

A little over . . . (*whispers the amount in BOISE's ear*)

PETER

Is there a washroom?

DEE points across the stage. PETER hops towards it.

BOISE

I offered Anstalt eighteen dollars a share. They wanted
twenty-two. They're trying to jack it up, before un-
loading.

DEE

(*to KILMAN*) Got a pencil?

*KILMAN almost absently hands it to her. She jams it into
PETER's heel.*

BOISE

Tell Anstalt I won't be free to meet them this month.

PETER

(*as if in pain*) A washroom?

BOISE

Let the stock hit nineteen and then start selling. Escalate

the lots one thousand, three thousand, five, whatever it takes to get them to back off.

KILMAN

(*to PETER*) You've peed your pants. (*exits*)

BOISE

See how exciting this market is?

BOISE immediately sits in the loveseat beside CLARE.

SCENE 13

BOISE and CLARE sitting on her Louis XIV loveseat.

BOISE

Don't most people just turn the pages?

CLARE

I can't read the print of paperbacks and hardcovers are too heavy. They tire my wrists.

BOISE

(*lifting up the book on CLARE's lap*) A biography of Henri the third?

CLARE

I'm just at the part where he wakes up out of a nightmare and executes all the animals in his zoo because he thinks they're going to kill him.

BOISE

(*bored*) Fascinating.

CLARE

Did you really knock on my door, after all these years, to discuss my reading habits?

BOISE

No.

CLARE

I expect you've heard about David.

BOISE

I'm sorry.

CLARE

I've been thinking of you lately, Frederick. I spend whole days rewriting the past.

BOISE

A bad habit.

CLARE

That's what I thought of you.

They share a smile.

CLARE

I've seen you a few times over the years, expect there's been more. Jilly pointed you out once. This was years ago, when you had the hook. She hadn't the foggiest who you were, but you gave her quite a fright.

BOISE

That was at least twenty-five years ago.

CLARE

David left me a bit of money, Frederick. Not a lot, but enough to survive. I know your chauffeur's waiting, so please don't bother to propose.

BOISE

Burnham Wood.

The lights are now up, so we see JILLSON at the pond. She's lying on her stomach with her hands at her side, studying a frog.

CLARE

Don't tell me you want to buy it?

BOISE

No. But there is a way of keeping it in the family.

CLARE

I don't want to keep it.

BOISE

It struck me that if you were to let me give you a mortgage on the property—say eight million dollars—

CLARE

I've never borrowed money in my life.

BOISE

Hear me out. If you in turn were to invest that money in a certain company—

CLARE

What company?

BOISE

A company which expanded rather carelessly. Naturally the markets have been harsh on it, but under the haze lie excellent fundamentals.

CLARE

Now I'm confused. Are you asking me for money?

BOISE

No. Clare, this stock's fallen as low as fifteen in the last ten months. It's currently hovering around twenty-one, but they've just brought in a new president and with a little sizzle it could top seventy.

CLARE

Honestly, I don't know anything about these things and I don't know why we're having this conversation. It's been thirty years and—

BOISE

Thirty-two.

CLARE

That world is dead.

BOISE

And so is David. Clare, I'm aware of your true financial situation.

CLARE

I'm sure you know the date of your own death.

BOISE

You've barely enough to maintain this understated elegance, and there certainly won't be any left over—

CLARE

I will not allow the conversation to turn in this direction.

BOISE

I just want to see that she'll be provided for.

CLARE

For the last time, Jillson is not your child. Not! Not! Not. The fact that she was premature proves nothing and I'll—

BOISE

I've hired her boyfriend.

CLARE

Peter?

BOISE

Yes.

CLARE

For Christ's sake !

BOISE

Someone has to take care of her—

CLARE

She is not a pet. She's quite capable of making her own way.

BOISE

But she isn't.

CLARE

Get a foster-child if you want, but stay away from Jill. She's had one father, and with his indulgence she's managed to shimmer through life like a ghost. It's only since his death that she's begun to materialize as a person. She was upset about the woods, but she accepted it, and she even volunteered to help at my soup kitchen.

BOISE

Don't you think that owning the woods might be the sort of responsibility she needs?

CLARE

I can see she's the only reason you came around.

BOISE

(*switching tactics*) I'm no good at declaring myself. It was childish to use Jill as a pretext, but in these matters I am childish.

CLARE

She is not yours.

BOISE

Not. The subject is closed. Clare, I'm offering to help you. If I thought you'd accept a cheque I'd do that.

CLARE

(*casually*) I suppose you know that last year David gave away eleven million—gave it anonymously—didn't even take the tax deduction. Somewhere up in heaven they're fitting the little shit out with wings. Now, when *you* go, hell will have to import extra fuel from Iran.

BOISE

Have you no fondness left for me?

CLARE

Don't turn puppy-eyed. I spent half a lifetime trying to decipher David's eyes. (*referring to her book*) I stick to the hard facts now—things I have no compunction about cutting out with a knife. Why did he give it all away? God, I can't bear the ambiguity of sensitive men.

PETER comes down the hill carrying a briefcase. JILL looks up, sees him, puts her finger to her lips telling him not to speak. She points to the ground. He sits beside her and studies the ground. We hear an occasional frog croaking and crickets in the distance.

BOISE, after pondering CLARE's remark, adopts a more direct approach.

BOISE

You'd make at least thirty million on this deal. That's

ten million each for you and Hillary, and enough for Jill to buy back the mortgage if she wants. Everyone wins.

CLARE

And what do you win?

BOISE

In the event of a takeover or a restructuring, I'd want your proxy—and you sell when I say.

CLARE

Only that?

BOISE nods yes.

CLARE

(*after a pause*) Is it criminal? David always said you were a criminal, Frederick. Are you?

BOISE

Nothing so ambitious. Lost my ambition when I lost you.

As BOISE gets out his phone book and dials, the lights fade to black and come up on PETER and JILL.

SCENE 14

JILL and PETER are at the pond, studying something on the ground.

PETER

Five crickets.

JILL

Six.

PETER

One, two, three, four—six. Six crickets, and one frog. All right, so why doesn't he eat them?

JILL

(*happy to teach*) I thought you'd never ask. The frog doesn't see them.

PETER

But they're right in front of his—

JILL

Frogs only see movement. As long as the crickets don't move, they're safe.

PETER

So, if I give this one a tap . . . (*he does*) Oops. Like I said, five crickets.

JILL

All right, Prince, you've had enough. Off you go. (*picks up the frog, kisses it, and places it in the pond*)

PETER

So, the cricket saves its life by playing dead.

JILL

Yeah, if it stops moving it disappears.

PETER

You've been standing still for a long time, Jill—

The phone in PETER's briefcase begins to ring.

JILL

Like most people, frogs only register dramatic changes.

PETER

(*reaching for his briefcase*) I should get that—

JILL grabs the briefcase and throws it into the pond.

My phone! Boise just gave me that phone.

JILL

Will you marry me, Peter?

PETER

(*staring into the pond*) My new phone . . .

JILL

I don't mean today, but I want to feel like we're heading towards something. I don't want to drift. And everything I thought was permanent—my dad, this place . . . they're gone.

PETER

(*confused*) Is this a proposal?

JILL

Will you?

PETER

(*smiling*) You don't detect a slight contradiction here? First you chuck my phone and then you ask me, me to . . . marry you?

JILL

(*cautiously*) Is there a contradiction in the way we feel?

PETER

(*laughs and embraces her*) I love you.

They kiss as BOISE puts down the phone in CLARE's space and walks to his office talking to PETER.

SCENE 15

*FREDDY BOISE is in his office. He begins talking to PETER, who
is still kissing JILL.*

BOISE

There comes a time, Peter, when idealism has to surrender to practicality. People change in direct proportion to
their self-interest. And in this game self-interest equals
profit. Something which is conspicuously absent from
your portfolio.

PETER

(*still kissing JILL*) You put up the money, I pick the
stock, and we have this discussion in three years. That
was the deal, Freddy. You hired me to do a job, and I'm
doing it.

BOISE

This isn't a job, it's an attitude, and you haven't got it.

PETER

Maybe not, but I wasn't—I may be over-educated, but
I'm not stupid. You're asking me to park this stock.

BOISE

To what? Pick up the phone!

JILL runs to her phone and begins to dial.

PETER

Why?

The phone in BOISE's office rings.

BOISE

Phone the goddamn Securities Commission. Phone! This
is legal and above—they'll tell you—phone! Christ,
they've been all over me and up me—they've even

talked to my proctologist. Phone. (*pushes a button on the speaker phone*) Yeah—?

JILL

Is Peter Malchuk there?

PETER

Hello, Malchuk.

JILL

Peter, I do love you. I do.

PETER

Can I, can I call you back?

JILL

I'll be here.

Lights in JILL's apartment fade.

PETER

(*hangs up*) I'm sorry, okay? I just know you have a lot of Life Products stock. I thought maybe you were over five per cent and didn't want to file a 13D.

BOISE

If I decide to cross five per cent, I'll file in neon and the stock will jump ten points. The street trusts my judgement, Peter. Get in now.

PETER

If you want to own this company, then I'm out. I could not in good conscience be a part—

BOISE

Who said anything about owning? I'm trying to help liberate the profits held by incompetent management.

Put the company on a diet, dress her up, find her a loving husband, and invite the small shareholders to the reception. I'm talking about a highly fucking moral endeavour.

PETER

But—

On cue KILMAN enters and hands BOISE three documents.

BOISE

Here's the numbers, price-earnings, break-up value, annual report. Just look at the numbers. All right? Could you at least do that for me?

PETER nods yes and exits

PETER

(*referring to KILMAN*) What's he run off, batteries? Or is he nuclear? (*exits*)

SCENE 16

BOISE's office.

BOISE

(*getting up and putting on his coat*) I'm off. Need a lift uptown?

KILMAN

I thought I'd wait around for Tokyo to open.

BOISE

Oh, Kilman—Sirroco Energy—do you know it?

KILMAN

I wouldn't think it's for you. My father used their pumps.

BOISE

Thought they made wind generators.

KILMAN

That too, but they've got a nifty water pump that is giving Jacuzzi ulcers. Low energy—half a horse pumps 200 gallons a minute. You could run a family of eight and a couple hundred head of cattle with that.

BOISE

No doubt. Look, I want you to see if that stock can undergo a correction.

KILMAN

Too closely held. There's—

BOISE

A few points, a rumour, enough to make someone think twice.

KILMAN

Done.

BOISE exits and once he's certain he's alone KILMAN presses the button which activates the bug in JILL's apartment. As he listens he undoes his tie and pours himself a drink.

SCENE 17

HILLARY and JILL in JILL's bedroom. HILLARY wears tennis whites.

HILLARY

It's an amazing penthouse. And when you're that high up, even the slums look like an impressionist painting.

JILL

But I don't want to move up.

HILLARY

It doesn't have to be a highrise. I've got the cute-ist house—

JILL

Hillary, we're content here.

HILLARY

All this contentment—pillow fights, late-night conversations, that post-orgasmic glow of yours—you know what your problem is?

JILL

I'm happy?

HILLARY

It's the sex, right?

JILL

It's not only sex, there's—

HILLARY

There's *only* sex, Jill. The rest is mortgage payments.

JILL

(*laughs*) You're looking for details, aren't you?

HILLARY

Who me?

JILL

It's nothing kinky.

HILLARY

But he's Catholic.

JILL

Sorry. It's just good sex . . . a little too good.

DEE enters BOISE's office. She stops to listen, unseen by KILMAN.

HILLARY

But?

JILL

Nothing. It's great.

HILLARY

But?

JILL

We're working on it. We have different sensitivities, okay?

HILLARY

He bangs like a jackhammer!

JILL

Hills! (*pause*) Sometimes I don't feel we're connecting because he's curled up in his brain and is afraid to come down into his body. . . . It's hard to please someone like that. I run my finger down his back, he doesn't feel it. I tickle his toes, he still doesn't feel it.

HILLARY

I slept with a jock like that. He wouldn't feel it if you dropped him in a garburator.

KILMAN laughs along with JILL, then sees DEE and smashes the button off. HILLARY and JILL go black. HILLARY exits.

KILMAN

What the—why are you here?

DEE

Forgot my dictation.

DEE pops a cassette out of a tape recorder as JILL heads to the woods.

DEE

I do type, you know. So, does this woman's sex life affect the stock market?

KILMAN

Oh, that. That was one of those radio dramas. I was waiting for the news.

DEE

Of course you were.

SCENE 18

JILLSON is at the pond digging a hole in which to plant the Russian olive which first appeared in scene 5. It's a hot day.
We hear a loud wind from a winter gale as KATHLEEN RILEY appears. She is dressed in a 1950s winter outfit and she walks across the water as if it were a sheet of ice, her head bowed into the wind. We hear a large cracking sound. She screams out "David!" and suddenly she disappears through the ice.
JILL rushes to her rescue, but it's too late.

JILL

Why didn't you save her? You could have saved her.

Suddenly we hear the voice of DAVID coming from behind the audience.

DAVID

(*voice over*) For Christ's sake, Jillson, would you stop about Kate Riley? It didn't happen. It didn't.

JILL looks around for a moment and then resumes digging.
We hear the sound of a lawn mower, off.
The next scene begins.

SCENE 19

KILMAN enters pushing the electric lawn mower across the top of the hill. This is a new KILMAN, more like a cowboy than a bureaucrat/spy. BOISE enters CLARE's space, and sits staring at a photo of young JILL.

KILMAN

Hi.

JILL

Do you mind?

KILMAN

What?

JILL

Do you?

KILMAN turns off the lawn mower.

JILL

Thank you. I was saying, would you mind not cutting the grass here? They just do it around the house—they—where are they? (*pause*) The crew? You're with Dennison's, aren't you?

KILMAN

. . . Yeah, well, I—they said go out to the Kidneys', so here I am.

JILL

The Kidneys are across the road. This is the Ashes'. (*resumes digging*)

KILMAN

This is the Ashes'?

JILL

Yes.

KILMAN

I guess you're an Ashe, then?

JILL

Guess I am. Sorry . . . (*puts out her hand*) it's Jillson.

KILMAN

(*shakes her hand*) Name's Newman. Paul Newman.

JILL

Like the actor?

KILMAN

Dad says I'm more like Alfred E. Newman.

JILL

Don't know him.

KILMAN

Cartoon guy. *Mad* magazine.

JILL

I'm afraid that stuff never appealed to me.

KILMAN

That's because you're an Ashe. I—sorry, didn't mean it like—just that, well—money people tend to be serious people and . . . am I getting in deeper?

JILL

(*smiling*) Yes, you are.

KILMAN

Always do. Meet a girl and they get up and walk away.
Could understand it when I was at home, we've got pigs.

JILL

I'm not going anywhere.

KILMAN

No?

JILL

No.

KILMAN

Can I ask you something?

JILL

Ask.

KILMAN

The place is up for sale, right?

JILL

That's what the sign says.

KILMAN

How come you're planting a tree?

JILL

It's a tradition. On special occasions, we plant a tree.

KILMAN

What's the occasion?

JILL

I don't want to be rude, but—

KILMAN

No problem. Here—let me get you a little mulch for that—(*exits off*)

JILL rolls her eyes. She puts the tree in the hole to see if it's deep enough. KILMAN re-enters with some rotten leaves.

KILMAN

Whoa—put the mulch in the bottom—Here, let me.

JILL concedes as KILMAN puts down the mulch, then some earth, then takes the tree from its pot or cuts some slits in its burlap, then puts the tree in the hole and shovels the dirt in with his hands, talking all the while. JILL gets a bucket and scoops some water from the pond.

KILMAN

Too bad you're selling. A thousand acres like this, they'll turn it into a subdivision in no time. You see what they did to the fourth line?

JILL

I'd rather not think about it.

KILMAN

Guess that's why you let the place fall apart. That garden's nothing but weeds, and the house—

JILL

The roof leaks, the furnace is broken, and we need a new well.

KILMAN

If you were staying, I could do you a well. Used to install them with my Dad and—

JILL

That's kind, but unfortunately we're not staying.

KILMAN

I take it you don't want to sell.

JILL

It's my mother. Until my dad died she'd forgotten all about this place.

KILMAN

(*finishing up, adjusts the tree stake*) It's for your dad, isn't it? The tree?

JILL

Yes.

KILMAN

(*looking out*) Russian olive makes a nice change from all this willow.

JILL

I prefer it.

KILMAN

(*noticing the tree stump*) What was the occasion behind this one? (*inspects the stump*)

JILL

My dad planted it when he was a boy. Apparently a little girl drowned here. He wouldn't tell me the whole story, but I remember him cutting it down on my tenth birthday.

KILMAN

Couldn't be this one. Not if he was a boy. It's too young.

JILL

Yes, it was.

KILMAN

When were you born?

JILL

Fifty-six.

KILMAN

(*quickly calculating*) Fifty-six plus ten—sixty-six. If the tree was cut down in 1966, you count back the rings—ten, fourteen, fifteen takes you back to fifty-one.

JILL

But then it would have been at least three or four years old before he planted it.

KILMAN

That would put it at 1954 or fifty-five.

JILL

You'd make a good detective.

KILMAN

What I can't figure is, why isn't it rotten?

JILL

It doesn't make sense. He told me he was a boy. He said he'd planted it the spring after she drowned.

KILMAN

It's like it was cut yesterday. (*noticing JILL is lost in thought*) Not bothering you, am I? 'Cause I could—

JILL

You're not bothering me, Alfred.

KILMAN

It's Paul, like the actor.

KILMAN exits uphill. JILL goes off to the side as CLARE enters.

SCENE 20

CLARE is talking to BOISE in her living room.

BOISE

Have you talked to them yet?

CLARE

I managed to get to Hillary. She said yes, but I haven't got my nerve up for Jill.

BOISE

I need an answer. I can't guarantee the price if—

CLARE

Enough said.

BOISE

I could chat her up?

CLARE

No.

BOISE

It could be very casual. She's coming to a sort of play my company's sponsoring next week.

CLARE

Pardon?

BOISE

Peter's not an "old boy." Somebody has to sponsor him. He needs to make contacts.

CLARE

And he's bringing Jill? The three of you?

BOISE

What could I say? He said Jill loves theatre. I couldn't—

CLARE

Does your scheming never stop? You knew she loves it.

BOISE

I didn't. Clare, it's just an evening out.

CLARE

Of course you always go to the theatre.

BOISE

I'm a patron of the—

CLARE

Frederick, you wouldn't know art if it paid dividends.

BOISE

I know it when I step in it.

CLARE

(*rapidly*) Does this play have a title? Is it a classic? Is the author dead or alive?

BOISE

They called it a "cultural event," so I assume he's dead.

CLARE

I demand to be invited. (*exits*)

The lights cross-fade with JILL's entrance to come up on PETER's office.

SCENE 21

PETER is talking on the phone in his office. In BOISE's space, JILL enters carrying a picnic basket. She is wearing the dress she wore in scene 2. He motions that he'll be right with her.

PETER

I won't buy your products, let alone the stock, until you guys change the packaging. C'mon, the tray's polystyrene, the wrap's plastic, the colour-dye is toxic. Great, with your help we'll all have fresh food at the apocalypse. Forget it, Vinny. (*bangs off the call, goes on to the next*) Yeah, Freddy, what about Sirroco Energy? You heard it fell! You mean you tried to make it fall. Don't dick with me, Freddy, the shorts went through Angel and the rumour started with Kilman's buddy at Drexel—yeah—I'm learning. So, stop wasting your money on my tuition. (*hangs up*)

JILL

(*turning*) What was that?

PETER

Freddy wants me in on this pesticide company. (*holds up the Life Products annual report*) He thought he could encourage me by trying to "tank" one of my stocks.

JILL

But isn't it his money? His loss?

PETER

It's a "paper loss." If I dumped Sirroco today and went into Life Products, his numbers predict at least a hundred and fifty per cent return. I'd make my one per cent and he'd make a fortune.

JILL

I don't know how you stand it.

PETER

It's only a matter of time before he starts believing his own publicity.

JILL

You believe that?

PETER

(*picking up a magazine*) Five pages in the *Financial Post*. Right here. "Peter Malchuk and the conversion of Freddy Boise."

JILL

Where did they take this picture of you?

PETER

On the roof.

JILL

You look like an angel. (*reading from the magazine*) "Says Peter Malchuk, a cleaner environment isn't going to come from protest or legislation—"

JILL & PETER

"—because governments never express the will of the people, only the market does."

PETER

I'm hot-hot-hot!

JILL

(*opens the hamper*) Champagne? (*hands him the bottle*)

PETER

You knew?

JILL

Hillary phoned. (*lapsing into French*) Aujourd'hui j'ai apporté du fromage—du Fontina et du Chaume—et une baguette, ainsi que des crevettes tigres et des asperges vinaigrettes . . . [Today I have Fontina and Chaume cheese and a French stick, and tiger shrimp with asparagus in a vinaigrette.] (*runs off and enters with a tree*)

PETER

(*begins to open champagne*) And a tree.

JILL

Un cadeau, pour mettre dans ton bureau. [A present for your office.]

PETER

It's great. What's with all the food? There's enough for ten.

JILL

Four. We're rushing off to this play tonight.

PETER

That's tonight?

DEE enters.

DEE

Peter, will you take a call on five? It's the chairman of Sirroco Energy. A benjamina—

PETER

Tell him I'll call tomorrow.

DEE

Is this your doing, Jill?

JILL

Guilty. (*spreads a picnic basket*)

DEE

Boise is allergic to them.

JILL

To benjaminas?

DEE

Anything green. Hold on, I'll get some water.
DEE exits. As PETER pops the cork, he calls after her.

PETER

And Dee—cups, glasses.

JILL

Is she your type?

PETER

What's that mean? You're my—

JILL

I'm sorry. It just popped out.

PETER

I wasn't looking at *them*.

JILL

(*coming on to him*) We could lock the door and play under your desk if you—
FREDDY enters.

BOISE

Peter, have you—my God, it's . . . of course it's you.

JILL

Is it?

BOISE

You're Jillson Ashe, of course you are. (*to PETER*) She's got her mother's skin.

JILL

She said I could borrow it.

BOISE

And she's droll.

PETER

Jill, this is Frederick Boise.

BOISE shakes her hand. JILL seems fixated on his artificial one.

BOISE

Freddy, I was at school with your father—before they threw me out. Truth is, it was your father who reported me for cheating. Follies of youth, ha-ha. But it was a good thing. He pushed, but I landed all right. Listen. I'm on the phone, actually—

PETER

The play starts at seven-thirty.

BOISE

The . . . ? Of course it does. And you were bringing a bite. We don't often dine al fresco on the sixty-fifth floor.

JILL nods yes.

BOISE

(*horrified*) Asparagus!

JILL stares at his hand.

Any fruit?

JILL

(*at the hamper*) There's some . . .

The lights shift as JILL takes out a copy of BOISE's arm; looks quickly around, but no one notices.

BOISE

(*volunteering*) Grapes?

JILL

Strawberries—I picked them up at—(*pulls strawberries from the hamper and puts the arm back in and the lights go back to normal*)

BOISE

Burnham Wood?

JILL nods yes.

BOISE

(*eating a strawberry*) Strange thing about strawberries, every time I eat one, I think I'm biting into a politician's nose. . . .

JILL doesn't find this as funny as PETER.

Burnham Wood, Shakespeare, right?

JILL

It's the way the wind blows the willows on the other side of the pond. They always appear as if they're moving towards you.

BOISE

Ah.

DEE enters. She is carrying a tray with four champagne flutes and a pitcher of water.

BOISE

Ah. Dee, why the pitcher?

DEE

Water for—

BOISE

(*startled*) My God, it's a tree!

PETER

From Jill.

BOISE

(*touching the leaves*) They're real.

JILL bursts out laughing at this.

PETER

You don't mind?

BOISE

(*coughing*) Not at all.

PETER

Champagne, Freddy?

CLARE enters.

CLARE

Did someone mention champagne?

BOISE

Clare!

CLARE

Don't think I've come to see you, Frederick. Peter's the man of the hour. Hello, Peter.

PETER

(*gives CLARE a kiss*) Clare.

DEE exits.

JILL

Hello, Mother.

CLARE

Now that's a nice outfit for a change.

JILL

Peter's choice.

CLARE

You're a good influence, Peter. A good influence on all of us. I read that article today, most impressive. He came off better than you, Freddy.

PETER

I don't think—

CLARE

You're modest, I like that. I have to confess, Peter, that I was apprehensive about this marriage, but now I must say I'm very impressed by my future son-in-law. Even Betsy Weir phoned to congratulate me. In fact, she's considering putting some money with you, and if she does, everyone will. Which is why the girls at the club want you to give a talk.

PETER

A speech? I'm not much for public—

CLARE

The *public* won't be there.

PETER

I'd need some time to—

CLARE

Five pages in the *Post*! Did you give him a reward, Freddy?

BOISE

Not yet.

CLARE

Well, I brought you a small token. (*hands him a small box*) It's not for telling the time, it's for the market. No matter where you are, just push the button and it displays the stock quotes.

PETER

Thanks. I love it.

BOISE

Let's have a toast, shall we? May your marriage prosper and your margins never be called.

They toast.

CLARE

Has she finally given you a date?

JILL

May.

CLARE

That's months from now.

PETER

(*playing with his watch*) Life Products closed up two points, to twenty-five and a quarter.

BOISE

Christ! Sorry. Peter, I've got Angel on hold. He's found a block of shares. You could have them at twenty-five.

PETER

Freddy, we've had this conversation.

JILL

I thought you put your money with Peter because you wanted to invest in ecologically sound companies.

BOISE

And this is.

JILL

Don't they make pesticides? (*opens the Life Products report*)

BOISE

Sure they do. But that stuff is made out of chrysanthemums. What could be more natural?

JILL

It says here that they're also into biotechnology.

BOISE

Yes. But if I have any say they'll get out. They don't have the capital for decent R&D.

JILL

And . . . did you read this, Peter? They're the "leading supplier of blood products from Africa." That's obscene.

BOISE

We would sell that division.

CLARE

You seem to be forgetting, Jill, that pesticides are needed to help grow food for a hungry world and I'm surprised to hear you calling Black blood obscene. I thought you were free of prejudice.

JILL

Right. Impoverished people selling their blood for food. What are they going to harvest next, their kidneys?

BOISE

The Indians already control that market.

JILL

These are human beings, not crops.

CLARE

By buying those shares we could save Burnham Wood.

JILL

Save it?

CLARE

Is your offer still on, Freddy?

BOISE

I'm holding three hundred and thirty-five thousand, at twenty-four dollars a share.

PETER

Which you just happen to have on the shelf?

CLARE

Frederick has very generously offered to loan me the money.

PETER

With the woods as collateral?

CLARE & BOISE

Yes.

BOISE

(*emphatically*) But I'll guarantee to turn over the mortgage in ten months, if the stock hasn't performed.

CLARE

(*taking out a deed*) Hillary has already signed. You do want to keep the woods?

JILL

Yes, but not—Peter, couldn't we invest with you?

PETER

I could never get his return.

CLARE

You have to decide, Jill, if you want your trees and the pond, all those things which let you hide from—I simply meant to say that sometimes in life you must do things which may appear distasteful in order to have or keep something you truly value.

JILL

Peter?

PETER

This really has to be your decision.

CLARE

There's no obligation. Mind you, it would give all of us, as well as the woods, some measure of security. But it is up to you, dear.

JILL

Peter?

PETER

I don't know if there's a right answer.

JILL

(*pauses*) All right. Do it.

CLARE

Sign there . . .

BOISE

This calls for another toast.

CLARE

. . . and there, dear.

JILL signs.

JILL

I . . . I'm going for a walk.

PETER

I'll go with you.

JILL

No. I'm fine, Peter. I'll meet you at the theatre. Honestly. (*kisses him*) Eat some food. (*exits*)

CLARE

(*to PETER*) I keep hoping she'll toughen up like her sister, but I'm afraid she'll always have her father's sensibilities. Now, I think you should get in on this stock.

PETER

I don't think so.

PETER sits down.

BOISE

You stick to your guns, Peter. That's good. I like it. But here's a word. There's the world you want to create and there's the one that exists. Look at that wind generator stock of yours. Four months and nothing. Why? Because that stuff is in the future—the future. But the money to create that future is right here—right now. It's in blood products from Africa. You don't have to hold the stock—you get in and out—but at year end the fund says "growth." And you start attracting the serious money which gives you the capital to take risks with wind generators.

CLARE

Peter, Jill needs someone who can make the tough decisions. And Burnham Wood is going to take considerably more money than you presently earn.

PETER

Okay! I'll commit four million. But it's off the books by year end.

BLACKOUT.

SCENE 22

Snap up the lights; we see what appears to be JILL lying on the floor, her head engulfed by the open jaws of the crocodile.
Two seconds pass.

BLACKOUT.

END OF ACT ONE

ACT TWO

The opposite of a correct statement is a false statement.
But the opposite of a profound truth may well be another
profound truth

NIELS BOHR

The heart has its reasons which the mind knows not.

BLAISE PASCAL

Again, if all movement is always inter-connected, the
new arising from the old in a determinate order—if the
atoms never swerve so as to originate some new movement that will snap the bonds of fate, the everlasting se-
quence of cause and effect—what is the source of the free
will possessed by living things throughout the earth?

LUCRETIUS

And so, without more circumstance at all,
I hold it fit that we shall shake hands and part,
You as your business and desire shall point you,
For every man hath business and desire,
Such as it is, and for my own part,
I will go pray.

HAMLET

SCENE 1

JILLSON, PETER, CLARE ASHE, and FREDDY BOISE enter the
theatre with the audience returning from intermission, or they sneak
in as latecomers after the house lights go down. The key is surprise.

They sit in the centre of the third or fourth row. The curtain is closed and the house lights go down. The curtain begins to go up and just as DEE becomes visible on the phone the curtain stops. DEE is surprised. She seems paralyzed by this actor's nightmare. Something is obviously wrong. The overture to the second act was Stravinsky's Rite of Spring—*we hear the technician desperately rewinding the tape.*

ANNOUNCER

(*on the public address system*) Ladies and gentlemen, there will be a slight delay, we have a . . . a technical problem. Please remain seated. The performance will resume shortly. Thank you.

The house lights come up. There is a pause long enough to allow the audience to begin making noise. DEE still doesn't know what to do. Suddenly a desperate hand shoots up from under the water of the pond.

JILL

(*jumping out of her seat*) Maybe it was the only thing to do, but I can't gloat over it! I can't be happy about buying it. And I'm certainly not grateful to him—

The hand sinks back into the pond.

CLARE

(*between clenched teeth*) Jillson.

PETER

Would you sit down?

JILL

(*over top of PETER's line*) I'm sorry. I'm such a drag because I can't pretend to be happy-happy-happy or banter with Betsy Weir's daughter, who is a lawyer or married a lawyer.

BOISE

Enough. For God's sake, sit down or get out!

JILL

(*rapidly, almost in one breath*) I don't just spend my days in the company of trees, I walk the streets and look at people.

PETER

C'mon. Let's go.

JILL

And I see the bag ladies and all the others who will pay the price for my greed. And I see my reflection in store windows—we're all good taste and good intentions. Christ, is there no end to the triviality we'll endure to keep from the inconvenience of actually living? I'm sorry to be so inconvenient, but I can't stand it!

JILL breaks away from PETER and runs out.
The house lights begin to fade as PETER runs after JILL through the side exit. He is followed by BOISE and CLARE.

CLARE

(*arriving near the side exit, sees someone in the audience*) Oh, Betsy. Hello. We were just—

CLARE faints and is caught by BOISE.

BLACKOUT. *The curtain rises rapidly.*

SCENE 2

DEE is talking on the phone in BOISE's office.

DEE

I don't want to hear what you think. . . . Because it's tedious to have this conversation every morning. . . . Listen, Angel, the next time you want to "chat" dial fantasy line. . . . But I don't want you to, honest. . . . When men say "honest," they mean pornographic. . . . Angel, would you stop saying you're hungry for me? Sex isn't a source of protein. . . . He's here. (*BOISE enters, she hands him the phone*) Angel.

BOISE

Thirty seconds . . . of course I know. Now we sit tight, and let them piss out their candles. And Angel . . . I think it's time to let our Japanese friends see the numbers, all right? (*he hangs up*) Kilman!

DEE

He's up at his dad's. What happened?

BOISE

Life Products put a halt on trading. Management is going to try to buy control at forty-seven dollars a share. (*rapidly, as DEE takes notes*) Dee, get on to the lawyers. I want them to (a) make certain there won't be any government problems if a foreign company enters the bidding. And (b) prepare to sue everybody. And I want the p.r. people to send faxes to every investment house telling them why Life Products is worth eighty dollars a share.

DEE

But if it's worth eighty, why was no one buying it at sixteen?

BOISE

(*rapidly*) Because at sixteen, it's a nickel game. At forty-seven, the stakes are too high for the real money not to play. A minute after the announcement, every investment banker in the country will start fantasizing about the millions in *fees* he can earn, if he can get a client to top forty-seven. "Forty-seven is a low-ball bid," they'll say. "Let's bid-em-up—c'mon, you've got to have balls to be a world-class player—bid-em-up." By five they'll have found some guy with a dick the size of a decimal point, and they'll make him feel like the last great stud. So he'll bid sixty, and then Life Products will have to unzip themselves and go sixty-five. Sure, at sixteen the numbers still said it was worth eighty—the parts are always worth more than the whole—but it's not really about numbers. It's about who's got the bigger dick. (*takes off his coat and lies on the desk*) Do my shoulders, would ya?

DEE

I should get on to—

BOISE

Dee, I need the fingers.

DEE begins to massage him as the next scene begins. The lights fade.

SCENE 3

JILL, HILLARY, and PETER in JILL and PETER's apartment. JILL wears her country clothes.

JILL

You don't get it, do you? Mum and Hillary split the cash and I'm supposed to feel good about protecting some wilderness from developers? I don't. I'm angry, for deluding myself into believing I'm doing something noble. I'm sorry, but I can't take my profit in the name of virtue. It's greed. Christ, I'm so greedy for it that I'll build a hundred justifications to have a place where I can escape the world, but every justification pulls me right back into it.

PETER

C'mon, you had a choice. You could have said you didn't want any part of it.

JILL

And I didn't hear you trying to talk me out of buying it. Where were you, Peter?

PETER

I'm not going to tell you what to do.

HILLARY

You could have voiced your objections at home.

JILL

I'm sorry, okay?

HILLARY

But you waited to get to the theatre.

JILL

I didn't.

HILLARY

Jillson, please. You've done it your whole life. When I was twelve you ruined my pajama party by convincing everyone that there was no point in shopping because they were going to drop the bomb.

PETER

Hillary, is that really to the point? The point is—

HILLARY

It is the point! You can be damn sure Mother thinks it's the point. When people go out in public they have to pretend to be having a good time. They're not supposed to talk about the world or their problems. They're supposed to forget. That's the etiquette. Look at Janet Farr.

JILL

She's dead.

HILLARY

(*rapidly*) Precisely. I saw her on the bridge, on the *bridge* for Christ's sake, and you know what she said? She said, "Hillary, I love your shoes." I love your shoes. . . . Ten minutes later she was pavement. But she understood' the etiquette. She didn't burden me by asking me the meaning of life. And every time I think of Janet, I don't think she's part of a sidewalk. I think—she had a way with compliments.

JILL

Are you saying I should jump?

PETER

She's not saying that at all.

HILLARY

You had no right to do that to Mother.

JILL

(*now sitting down in front of the bed*) If she'd only admit that we bought the stock to make an obscene amount of money, I'd shut up. But no, she has to pretend there's something altruistic behind it.

HILLARY

(*taking a shovel from beside the bed, she begins to dig up the set and pour the dirt on JILL as she speaks*) You move from one shelter to the next. I thought when you decided to marry Peter you were voting to join the rest of us. But that isn't it at all, is it? He's just replaced Dad. He's another refuge you can run to after throwing stones.

PETER

(*takes over digging from HILLARY and speaks tenderly to JILL as he proceeds to bury her*) Throw stones.

I love you for getting indignant, but there's no point in screaming if you're not going to work for change. I watched my father dying of black-lung and Mom snap when she couldn't cope, while the mine owner retired to his château in France. So I went on protest marches and wrote letters to politicians, because that was all I could do. But now, I'm at the table. I've got corporations asking *me* to tell them what they have to do to clean up their act.

KILMAN, unnoticed by all, enters wearing a blindfold and apparently dowsing for water with a willow branch. He roams freely throughout the scene.

JILL

You think because you convince some corporations to adapt a new way of packaging profit that the world is changing? It isn't.

PETER

We're making progress.

JILL

And that's good, is it?

PETER

Of course it's—

JILL

And where is this good? It's somewhere in the future. It's something we're progressing towards! By the time we get there, people like Boise will have seduced us out of whatever humanity, whatever decency we might have possessed. That world out there, the pollution, the pesticides, the garbage, the bloody garbage—it's us, that's the mirror I'm looking into, and even if we wrap it in a new green dress, it's still rotten. It's us, it's all the tiny compromises that pile up like trash. And if we don't start changing our values, really ripping them up and starting anew, looking at ourselves, our feelings, and how we lost sight of—

HILLARY

Fuck this! I'm leaving. She's all yours, Peter. (*goes to exit, then stops*) You think people are interested in feelings? People are interested in what you do—*do*—in the world! That's what people are interested in. People say, "What did you *do* today?" and I say, "I sold a house and made $43,000 commission." That is an event. Feeling is *not* an event, it is *not* an accomplishment, and it is not something people want to know. Good night.

PETER picks up HILLARY's magazine and stares at JILL as KILMAN starts talking.

SCENE 4

At the woods, KILMAN a.k.a. NEWMAN, wearing a blindfold, continues dowsing for water with a willow branch. The lights come up on another day in BOISE's space. DEE wears a new blouse. She massages BOISE, who begins to snore.

KILMAN

You look like your voice. Did you know that? Never imagined I could see someone with my eyes closed, but when you speak I—

JILL

Where was I?

KILMAN

(*after a beat*) Uh . . . something about trying to measure the exact position—

JILL

—of an electron?

KILMAN

Right.

JILL

(*animated by teaching, she gets up out of the dirt*) I can't measure its position without my act of measuring affecting its momentum. And if I affect its momentum I change its position.

KILMAN

(*confused*) What?

JILL

I'm not being clear. Imagine instead of position or momentum, we're talking about heads or tails.

KILMAN

So the electron is a coin?

JILL

Well, *like* a coin. . . . So I throw it up in the air . . . now is it heads or tails?

KILMAN

(*as if seeing the coin flip*) It's flipping all over the place. I don't know if it's heads or tails until I see it land.

JILL

So while the coin is in the air it's both heads and tails. It's only your act of observing it which forces it to be one or the other. You see, because we are suddenly part of the equation the whole idea of the "objective" observer, or of some "objective" reality for that matter, falls apart. It's impossible to talk objectively.

A shiny coin falls from the sky. JILL picks it up. KILMAN doesn't notice this. JILL stares at PETER, who's reading on the bed. PETER exits.

KILMAN

Jill.

JILL

Sorry I—

KILMAN

You disappeared on me.

JILL

It struck me that I always call tails while everyone else calls heads. Tails never turns up. It's as if everyone's using two-headed coins.

KILMAN

You've lost me now. I could get the physics, but—

JILL

You know how sometimes you get a feeling? It may not be rational, it may just be an intuition, but it feels right? And then somehow you forget it, or it gets drowned by everyone else saying the opposite?

KILMAN

Calling heads?

JILL

(*nods yes*) So you don't say anything, you just go along. Maybe there just aren't words for it. But that doesn't mean it can't be understood.

KILMAN

Like falling in love?

JILL

(*evading the implications*) Even something like . . . well, like dowsing.

KILMAN

A guy and a stick. What's to understand?

JILL

Not a lot in isolation. On your own, neither you nor the stick will find water, but together—

KILMAN

I still haven't.

JILL

You said it works for your dad. And it worked for me.

KILMAN

Okay. One more time.

He puts the blindfold on her.
Meanwhile, certain that BOISE is asleep, DEE takes a set of keys from his pocket and opens a drawer which contains a company cheque-book.
After inserting a pen in BOISE's artificial hand, DEE pulls on the thumb and it starts moving. She places the cheque-book under the hand and gets it to sign several cheques.

JILL

But we wouldn't really know if there was water unless we drilled.

KILMAN

C'mon. It's fun. One more time.

He hands her the dowsing rod, leads her away, and then spins her about.

JILL

(*after a bit*) Somehow I've lost sight of that other side. I thought Peter was the perfect balance so I just let myself fall into this life with him.

KILMAN

Keep going and you'll fall into the pond.

JILL

My mom's always saying that I do things by half and here I've done it again. I'm living off Peter and keep coming up here.

KILMAN

You're way off.

JILL turns in the opposite direction.

JILL

Everyone thinks that I just want to lie by the pond and feel the sun on my face, but if I love someone, if I'm supposed to have a connection to someone . . . shouldn't it feel at least as right as the sun on my face?

Meanwhile, DEE rips out the signed cheques and puts them down her bra.
Suddenly the dowsing rod bends dramatically. JILL reacts as if she's just burnt her hands.

JILL

(*dropping the rod*) Shit!

KILMAN

(*aiding her*) You all right?

JILL

(*shaking her hands*) Feels like they're on fire.

KILMAN

(*taking her hands*) They're bleeding. (*takes out a handkerchief*)

JILL

It's a scratch.

KILMAN

Hold this. (*handing her the handkerchief*) We should get something on them.

JILL

I'm fine. Don't worry. (*excited*) Now are you convinced? I found the same spot twice.

KILMAN

That's water all right and it's real close to the surface. Twenty-five, thirty feet, tops.

JILL

Sure it's there?

KILMAN

(*holding her hands*) Would these hands lie?

JILL

And close to the surface?

KILMAN

(*moving in*) Practically bursting out. It's close. Very close.

He goes to kiss her, but JILL evades his mouth as PETER appears out of nowhere.

JILL

(*stopping herself*) I shouldn't have said those things about Peter. I . . . Christ, I've got to go.

As JILL exits, she drops KILMAN's handkerchief. KILMAN lingers for a bit trying to figure out what has just transpired. He notices the handkerchief, picks it up, examines the blood on it, and freezes in place.

SCENE 5

DEE has placed BOISE's keys back in his pocket but is unable either to stop the hand or to get the pen out of it.

PETER

Fred. . . .

DEE

(*startled*) You scared me. (*pause*) He's sleeping. (*noticing PETER looking at the moving hand*) I was . . . just started moving. (*walking past she pulls the pen out of the hand*)

PETER

I'll come back (*goes to exit*)

BOISE wakes up with a start.

BOISE

Ah, Peter, the man I wanted to— (*noticing his moving arm*) What's this?

DEE

I was doing your shoulder and it started. (*shrugs*)

BOISE

(*pulling on the thumb, stops the hand*) I read your memo, Peter.

PETER

And you agree?

BOISE

I don't like things in writing, and I don't agree. Life Products put out an offer at forty-seven and the market raced right past it.

BOISE is up now and putting on his jacket. We notice that DEE is hiding the cheque-book behind her back.

PETER

Yes, but this new bid from the Japanese is all cash.

BOISE

Shoma Chemical has deeper pockets than fifty-nine dollars a share. It's still too low. (*noticing KILMAN, who is still frozen*) What have you got?

KILMAN

(*hesitant to speak, he motions for BOISE to join him away from the others*) The initial test of the blood on the handkerchief looks positive—

BOISE

(*happy*) She is? She is?

KILMAN

(*quietly*) It just means your blood types are compatible. He still has to do the genetic fingerprinting, but he's fairly sure.

BOISE

Fairly sure? What kind of fucking scientist is he? I want to know! (*turning to PETER and DEE*)

KILMAN

Could you two leave?

BOISE

Wait outside, Peter.

DEE and PETER exit, DEE having somehow managed to get the cheque-book back in its place.

KILMAN

I think there's a resemblance.

BOISE

Certainty! What's going on here? I gave my goddamn blood! Are they reading the entrails of some pig? You tell the son-of-a-bitch to find a bigger microscope. I don't care how much he has to enlarge it, but I want the absolute-irreducible-fucking-truth, and I want it to-day, on this desk on a piece of paper I can staple to the woman's heart!

KILMAN

If you tell Jill—

BOISE

Kilman, I meant the mother.

KILMAN

Oh. I only meant you'd really be starting something. You'd have to explain how I got her handkerchief out of her garbage and—

BOISE

Don't worry about Jill and start listening to the street. All right?

KILMAN nods yes.

BOISE

(*walking him out*) And run a check on Dee for me?

KILMAN

Dee?

BOISE

Just do it, would ya? Her fingers make me nervous. Peter.
(*motions to PETER to enter*)

PETER enters as KILMAN exits.

BOISE

Where were we?

PETER

I've got a bad feeling about the whole deal.

*BOISE puts his arm around PETER's shoulder They amble across the
stage, passing JILL, who has re-entered and now sits by the pond.*

BOISE

Feelings? You can't let feelings enter into it. This is
about price, and if that's beyond your grasp I suggest
you go back to your terminal and stop thinking you
have the skills to made decisions on your own. You
don't. The markets are too complicated. We're piloting
the economy, Peter. We have to rely on the objectivity
of computers, and they say it's worth eighty.

PETER

It seems to me they caused the last crash.

BOISE

Don't be punk. If you bail out now what happens to all
the small shareholders I'm fighting for? To Jill, and the
woods? There's a hell of a lot more to consider than your
bad feelings. . . . Fuck.

PETER and BOISE walk into the wings.

SCENE 6

*JILL is down by the pond. After a pause KILMAN launches himself
out of the water, scaring the shit out of JILL. He is wet and in his
underwear.*

JILL

(*after reacting*) That wasn't funny. That . . . (*she starts laughing*) . . . that really wasn't funny.

KILMAN

It's freezing. (*starts running on the spot*)

JILL

(*smiling*) It's September.

KILMAN

You *did* find water—and—the well's in.

JILL

You're making this up.

KILMAN

Am I?

JILL

When could you have done it? Drill, test—

KILMAN

(*off*) Last week. (*reappearing with a garden hose with a watering gun attached*)

JILL

I bet there isn't a drop of water in that hose.

KILMAN

How much?

JILL

You're lying.

Honestly. Took about five hours. Then I went fishing.

JILL

Here?

KILMAN

Yeah.

JILL

You're in deeper, Newman.

KILMAN

It's true.

JILL

There's no fish in the pond. Hasn't been since I was a girl.

KILMAN

Just like there's no water in the hose.

JILL

Right.

KILMAN sprays her with the hose.

Ahh! We've got water. I can't believe you. Are there really fish?

KILMAN

Caught a three-pound trout last week. (*drops the hose as they look in the pond*)

JILL runs back, grabs the hose, and sprays him. They kiss, long and passionately, and eventually wrestle for control of the hose. JILL runs off. KILMAN starts to pursue her with the hose.

SCENE 7

PETER, in a new suit, is talking to BOISE. A very playful but silent KILMAN and JILL run into the scene. KILMAN now has the hose. JILL hides behind PETER (as if he were a tree) to avoid being hit by the water.

BOISE

A week ago you wanted to sell at forty-five. Now it's fifty-one and climbing. What do you want to be, a smart money manager or a Polish joke?

PETER

(*angered but not rising to the insult*) Freddy, I'm supposed to be running an ecological fund. I can't show this stock in my portfolio at year-end.

KILMAN, trying to spray JILL, sprays PETER.

BOISE

Don't sweat.

JILL runs out. KILMAN runs after her.

BOISE

Kilman!

KILMAN

(*abruptly changing his manner*) Sir?

BOISE

What's Shoma Chemical's stake in Life Products?

KILMAN

They came out of nowhere with eleven per cent, and yesterday they filed again at seventeen per cent.

BOISE

And the Life Products management?

KILMAN

Neck and neck.

BOISE

Stay on it.

KILMAN runs out in pursuit of JILL.

Peter, this a race for control. And whoever wants to get it is going to have to bid at least seventy. And if they stay neck and neck, one of them might even pay a premium for our stock. Remember, between you, Clare, and me, we hold seven-point-five per cent.

JILL and HILLARY walk through the scene on the way to JILL's space. HILLARY wears a new outfit. DEE enters with some papers for BOISE to sign.

HILLARY

Remember all that stuff in geography about the world being ninety per cent water?

JILL

Two-thirds.

HILLARY

Whatever, most of us are floating on the surface. We know there's more to it, but why not catch the rays and eat a little soft shell? You, Jillson, are drowning. You've got a lifeline in Peter. Don't blow it.

PETER

(*to BOISE*) All right.

HILLARY

This is the first guy who doesn't mind you swimming all day.

As JILL gets into bed, the conversation continues, but we don't hear it.

PETER

Another couple of weeks, but that's it.

BOISE

(*relieved*) Finally.

Enter KILMAN. He's still in his underwear, still pursuing JILL. She sees him and invites him under the covers.

PETER

(*goes to leave*) Never again, Freddy! I don't want to hear about deals like this. I'm serious. I've stayed away from the hard questions, but don't think I don't know the answers. (*exits*)

DEE exits.

BOISE

(*to no-one*) What was that? (*pause*)

HILLARY is now on the phone and JILL has gotten into bed. HILLARY is smoking.

HILLARY

No, it's a fabulous place. French kitchen, Italian bathroom. Even the dust is imported.

BOISE

(*looking up from his work, to KILMAN*) Tell me something I don't know.

KILMAN

(*suddenly back in the office*) Life Products is trying to get Shoma Chemical to give them a standstill agreement. (*heads back to JILL*)

HILLARY

Four bedrooms—

BOISE

That won't happen.

KILMAN

Why?

HILLARY

Three million, and they'll throw in the maid.

BOISE

I'll worry about the Japanese, you concern yourself with Life Products. Could we get a wire into their boardroom?

KILMAN

Done. (*picks up the phone and dials, turns upstage. His movements mime HILLARY's*)

BOISE's space goes black.

HILLARY

Tomorrow. Got to go. (*hangs up*) Where was I?

JILL

Who are you?

HILLARY

Unfortunately, your sister.

JILL

Sorry to be such an embarrassment.

HILLARY

I'm trying to teach you some survival skills, Jillson. Hold on to Peter. I'm serious, Jill. Don't go back to the woods, don't see the water man again. And for God's sake, don't tell Peter. You'll end up on the bottom, Jill. You'll be kelp, Jill, kelp. (*she stubs her cigarette out in BOISE's ashtray as KILMAN hangs up the phone*)

BLACKOUT.

SCENE 8

A pinspot illuminates a glass case filled with water. A woman with her back to us is struggling to break free, but she is under ice a foot thick. She struggles to breathe between the ice and the water. This might also be done as a film projection. Five seconds pass.

BLACKOUT.

SCENE 9

The lights come up on JILL as she bolts up out of bed and walks over to BOISE's space, which has now been transformed into JILL and PETER's dining room. PETER is working late. He has some brandy. JILL's purse is also on the table. JILL takes a sip of brandy from PETER's glass.

PETER

Are you all right?

JILL

(*nods no*) I thought by getting engaged I was creating some order in my life. Hillary makes it seem so neat and tidy. Everything frozen in place. Things seemed solid, then suddenly you fall through the ice.

PETER

Everyone has doubts.

JILL

(*surprised*) You do?

PETER

(*pushing away from the table, motions for her to sit on his lap. She doesn't move*) Sometimes I wonder, am I actually making a difference? (*indicating his paperwork*) Are my numbers morally superior to theirs? The hot kid on the street? A big success? That's what the papers say, but I play with the same numbers, work the same deals, and at three in the morning with the light shining on you, just like that, I'm still sitting at the table. Is this a better life? (*pause. JILL walks over and begins massaging his shoulders*) If you want to win, to succeed, you have to play the game—but it's their game, their rules. I'm winning, Jill, but some nights, some nights even I can't convince myself it makes a difference. (*smiles*) That's your influence.

PETER sees JILL is crying.

Jill . . . Jill. . . . What is it?

JILL

You're making it so confusing. I do love you, Peter. I do.

PETER pulls her down.

PETER

I love you too. (*pause*) Is something—

JILL

(*getting up*) Sit there, will you?

PETER

(*sits back down*) You're not going to blame me for something I did in your dream, are you? I've got an alibi.

JILL

Remember. I told you about dowsing, about Paul, the water man?

PETER

The one who came on to you?

JILL

(*nods yes*) He kept coming up to the woods. I knew he was interested. I never thought I was . . . but it happened.

PETER

It? It? (*writes as if not listening*)

JILL nods.

PETER

You and him?

JILL nods.

It just happened? "Hi, baby, want to . . . ?" (*calming down*) It doesn't happen like that. A lot of things have to be wrong. There has to be a lot wrong with us and, and . . . what was so wrong, Jill?

JILL

There's a lot right . . . but . . . something happened today . . . a connection that I wish . . . that I wanted to happen between you and me . . . but it hasn't.

PETER

You love him?

JILL

I don't. No, it's not love.

PETER

Country boys are better in the sack.

JILL

Peter.

PETER

I'm sorry. I'm trying to be—I'm going to call him. (*grabs her purse, dumps it out onto the tray, grabs her phone book*)

JILL

There's no point. I don't have his number.

The pace becomes rapid.

PETER

He beat me! Some guy bested me and he's out there laughing at—

JILL

Nobody beat you!

PETER

How do you want me to react, Jill? I can't understand what's happening here. Did you plan it? Tell me.

JILL

He appears—

PETER

Out of nowhere. He kissed, just came up and kissed—

JILL

I want to be with you, Peter.

PETER

I need to know the details. If I know the details, the facts, maybe I can turn them into something I can't understand.

JILL

Frightening. I was standing there and . . .

KILMAN appears, comes up behind JILL and cradles her from behind, kissing her neck, unseen by PETER.

And it wasn't as if he was physically there at all. He could have been a ghost, because he just passed right through me. His whole body passed right through my skin, and it was like he punctured some sadness and I started to cry and cry. And I'd never been so happy to cry, just cry.

PETER

(*interjecting with disdain*) Crocodile tears.

JILL

. . . and feel like there was someone who understood. But who was it? I was so frightened because I couldn't see who . . . Paul was there, Dad, you, even Boise.

KILMAN withdraws into the darkness and JILL finds herself holding his arm, which is the same as the one BOISE has.

PETER

Boise?

JILL

Images kept flashing, and I kept crying and—

PETER

Because you were guilty.

JILL

Peter, I'm trying to explain.

PETER

Guilty!

JILL

Would you stop reducing it to sin?

PETER

(*rapidly*) How the hell do you expect to build any meaning into life if you can't stand and say *no*? Do you have any idea what I go through every day? Surrounded by vicious people, by greed and temptation?

BOISE enters CLARE's space.

I let your mother and Boise talk me into buying that stock.

JILL

You didn't.

PETER

(*over top of JILL's line*) Because of you, I betrayed every investor who put money with me believing I ran an ecological fund. I put my love for you above my own ethics.

JILL

I'm not up there.

PETER takes the brandy and pours it on the contents of JILL's purse.

PETER

You think I don't have desires? That Dee, that secretary. I wanted to, I could, I could have *had* her, but I didn't. I kept faith with you.

JILL

Please, take me off this cross.

PETER lights the contents of the purse on fire.

BOISE

(*as CLARE enters*) He sends her up to the woods to think about it. As if all she'd done was refused to eat her peas.

CLARE

Well, he must be very confident she'll return. I think it shows strength of character on Peter's part.

BOISE

Please, Clare, don't read character into what is obviously imbecility.

PETER

(*quietly staring at the flames*) It was your goodness. You gave me something to . . . I try to do the right thing. . . . (*softly*) A woman falls down in the street, I help her up. So would you, but you just do it. Not because it's right—no priest told you—you just do it. I always felt as long as you were there I had this kind of moral safety net. And look what's happened, what you've done. Christ, what *I've* done.

PETER and JILL stare at the flames as the next scene begins.

SCENE 10

As PETER and JILL watch the contents of her purse burn, the lights come up on BOISE and CLARE in her living room. She pours him a drink.

CLARE

Perhaps he understands her better than—

JILL exits

BOISE

He should have thrown her out on her ass. Throw her out, she'll come to her senses.

CLARE

Personally, I've lost faith in her ability to change. She wants a relationship to come gift-wrapped and perfect. She simply cannot accept that a relationship is a life's work. It ends, and the best you can say is "I survived."

BOISE

(*pouring another drink*) You make it sound like a car accident.

CLARE

Well, it is. It's more like . . . remember you took me to the exhibition, that ride?

BOISE

The bumper cars!

CLARE

More like that.

BOISE

Ninteen fifty-four.

CLARE

That was when your father went bankrupt.

BOISE

Is that what you remember? That's when I lost the arm.

JILL re-enters and packs a loose suitcase, then straightens the bed. PETER is in his office, trying to work but unable to concentrate.

CLARE

You know, I rather miss the hook.

BOISE

Never understood you, Clare . . . . The arm didn't bother you.

CLARE

I suppose that was surprising to some people. But remember, I had a three-legged dog.

BOISE

(*laughing*) Thanks a lot.

CLARE

I did love you back then, didn't I?

BOISE

Not enough to marry.

CLARE

You're the one who abandoned me for some stock swindle.

BOISE

A man's got to eat, but if I'd known about Jill I'd—

JILL exits upstage as HILLARY enters and leans over the headboard of the bed.

CLARE

Would you stop it about Jill. She's nothing to do with you.

BOISE

(*taking out a file*) Let's stop talking about *our* history as if she isn't a part of it. I'm tired of pretending she isn't.

She is. She's my child, Clare. And if you want to prove it in court, I will. Read this report. Go on. Read it. Genetic fingerprinting. You give these scientists a hair or a drop of blood and they can tell you the damn licence plate of the car she was conceived in.

PETER snaps a pencil and goes to lie on the bed. HILLARY looks down on him.

CLARE

(*throws the report into the wings*) She's not some company you can take over! She's—

BOISE

My child! And unless you want me to tell her, you bloody well better calm down and listen to me! I feel responsible for her—

CLARE

I knew that you knew and as long as you didn't say it, it was all right. It was. It was all right. But you have to own everything.

BOISE

(*lovingly*) I didn't know. Not for certain. Never for certain. (*pause*)

The lights begin to fade.

When they amputated the arm they warned me about phantom pain. I get these sensations in the arm, my missing arm. It's not there, but I can feel it. I can clench it, wave it, but it's not there. Business lets me use the pain. It keeps me ruthless, and as long as I keep my hand in the flame, keep focused on the deals, the pain is endurable. Nights when it gets real bad, I do this visualization thing they taught me. I accept the hand as being still there and pretend I'm walking down the street, with you holding one hand and Jill holding the other. Take my hand, Clare.

PETER takes HILLARY's hands.

CLARE

An arm caused all that, did it? I hate to think what you'd say if you were circumcised.

The lights fade on BOISE and CLARE and come up on PETER and HILLARY.

SCENE 11

HILLARY

See, the way I see it, and Ronji sort of gave me some perspective on this, is that everything has to happen. One day you're the cuckold, next Don Juan. I've done some shitty deals, but if I don't do them in this life, I'll only have to do them in my next incarnation.

PETER

That sounds like a licence to kill.

HILLARY

I'm just saying there's no point in blaming yourself for what happened.

PETER

But I do.

HILLARY

Let it go.

PETER

I need my guilt. It gives me boundaries.

BLACKOUT.

SCENE 12

BOISE appears hovering in the darkness behind PETER's bed. He carries a lit blowtorch and his voice is amplified. PETER is having a nightmare.

BOISE

Listen, it's not the light. It's the sound, the hissing—the intensity. Listen to the flames, Peter, and imagine what we could accomplish if we could endure their intensity. Man, the superior being. Ha, we cry if we stub our toe. We'll never evolve as long as we're chained to our emotions. The little progress we've made has been made by a few of us, who, with the courage of Prometheus pick up the flame, while the rest are content to watch shadows dance on the cave wall.

We hear the occasional buzz of an office intercom.

Survival is the privilege of those who can adapt. Look at the flame, Peter! I said stare at it—you little son-of-a-bitch. You think you can put out the fire, a fire that's been smouldering for a hundred years, a fire we lit in the industrial revolution and will not be put out? Not with all your laws or wind generators or biodegradable diapers.

A nude KILMAN and JILL surface in the pond. They're locked in an embrace.

Punks like you are dinosaurs in the new ice age. Look at the flame, Peter. Feel it. Is it hot or cold? Your senses can't even tell you that—they just want to flee. But there's nowhere to go. We can't save the environment! Are you listening, you little prick? We have to change. And we are! (*holds his artificial hand over the flame*) Look at it. Am I a freak, some chance mutation? No. Look at it! This is why we will endure.

KILMAN and JILL disappear.

Step by step we're climbing up, hand over hand we're pulling ourselves free of our bodies. Free of desire, of need. We're becoming our own creation, Peter, a creation which will need no food, no water, no air, no heartbeat. This flame burns eternal and so will we.

SCENE 13

PETER rolls onto the floor in a cold sweat as DEE enters. The scene is frantic.

PETER

(*still dreaming*) Don't burn me! Jesus, God, don't—

DEE

Peter—Peter, are you all right?

BOISE disappears as PETER bolts up.

PETER

(*as if winded*) Dee! I thought the flames. . . . Jill was there and he. . . . (*turns to see BOISE*) I couldn't move.

DEE

Can I get you something? Some aspirin?

PETER

I wanted to move, but every step was a judgement and every judgement a step closer to hell.

DEE

Some Valium?

PETER

Boise had this torch, and—

DEE

I've been buzzing you, you were supposed to be at Sirroco Energy.

PETER

(*looks at watch*) My interview—

DEE

I said you were on your way.

PETER

(*jumps up and searches frantically*) I—where's the phone book?

DEE

(*hands him the book, which was right in front of him*) Are you sure you're all right?

PETER

Yeah, yeah, I just haven't been sleeping. (*looking up a number*) Jill and I . . . well, she's moved up to the country for a while. (*dials*)

DEE

I'm sorry.

PETER

Would you do something for me?

The phone in CLARE's space begins to ring.

DEE

I've called the plant doctor. He's sending over a prescription.

PETER

(*seeing DEE looking at the tree*) You could have it if you want.

DEE

Sure.

CLARE enters from an unexpected direction into PETER's office.

CLARE

Hello, Peter. I thought I'd drop by and see how you were bearing up. (*kisses him*)

PETER

(*hanging up*) I was just calling you.

CLARE

Really? I love coincidences, they're so unexpected. Now I wanted to say—

PETER

(*writing as he talks*) Clare, I'm sorry to be abrupt, but I'm running late. I was calling to tell you I'm getting out of Life Products and I think you should too. (*hands her a piece of paper*) Call Angel.

DEE

But Boise said it'll top eighty.

PETER

(*quietly to CLARE*) Do you think it was coincidence that we both bought the day before the first announcement?

CLARE

(*to DEE*) Is Mr. Boise in?

DEE nods no.

PETER

I'm not saying he didn't have good intentions.

CLARE

Peter, I appreciate your concern, but—

PETER

If we sell when he does, some stock watcher is going to notice we're piggy-backing on his trades. If this deal sours—

CLARE

I've every confidence that anything you might deduce Freddy has already anticipated. Well, I should let you get to your meeting. If you need any hand-holding about Jill, call.

CLARE exits.

PETER

(*stunned by CLARE's departure*) She didn't hear it. You try to help and—

DEE

She's right about Boise. He plans for everything.

PETER

(*throwing some notes into his briefcase*) Dee, could you get on to Angel and tell him to sell all my stock "at the market." I don't want to talk to Freddy about it, I just want out. Could you do that for me? (*hands her the tree*)

DEE

For a dead tree?

PETER

For a friend?

DEE

Hey, it's your career.

PETER

It's my fund!

DEE

All right. I'll do it—because I like your feet.

PETER

(*kisses her on the cheek*) I'm out.

BOISE enters and sits in the swivel chair.

DEE

(*going after PETER*) Better take your coat. Boise won't let you past security after this.

PETER re-enters and takes his jacket off the back of his chair.

PETER

I'm not coming back.

They disappear. CLARE enters her space.

SCENE 14

BOISE is at his desk.

BOISE

Kilman!

CLARE is back home staring at the phone as KILMAN runs past.

KILMAN

Sir? (*sees Jill enter and is drawn towards her. They meet at the bed*)

BOISE

Have we got that bug on the Life Products board meeting
tomorrow?

KILMAN

Uh . . . no.

BOISE

Why?

KILMAN

Their boardroom has the same kind of detection system
we use.

BOISE

Yeah.

KILMAN

They just installed it.

BOISE

Has the room got windows?

KILMAN

(*on the bed kissing JILL*) Yes.

BOISE

Didn't you tell me a man with a parabolic mike could
stand on the roof opposite and hear me breathe?

KILMAN

If conditions are right.

BOISE

Well, do I have to *do* it for you? What's gotten into you?

I need to know if Life Products can top seventy-seven.

KILMAN

I'll get right on it.

BOISE

I think this one's going to eighty, Kilman.

KILMAN

We'll find out tomorrow.

BOISE

(*walks over to the bed and takes out a cigar*) We pulled it down from forty-five to fifteen and we'll ride it back up to eighty. Better than pissing on your boots. Isn't it?

KILMAN

(*still kissing, lights BOISE's cigar*) I suppose so.

BOISE

You bet it is. And Kilman, next time you're home—ask your father who might have put in a new well at Burnham Wood.

KILMAN

(*rolls off JILL*) He's out of the business but—

BOISE

You're looking for a young man, someone who "dowses." Is that the word?

KILMAN

Yes.

BOISE

Find him. And, I don't know, tell him he's won a trip.

Round the world. For one. I'll pay. And Kilman, the contest rule is that he goes, disappears, immediately.

KILMAN gets off the bed, does up his zipper, and exits.

SCENE 15

We hear the sound of a baby crying. From behind the bulrushes a baby emerges. It floats towards JILL, propelled by the current. She picks up the child, wrapped in a blanket, and heads to her mother's.

CLARE is talking to ANGEL as JILL enters. We hear music from the French court playing quietly in the background.

CLARE

Angel? Clare Ashe. I've decided to . . . Clare Ashe. . . . Correct. I've decided to sell my Life Products stock. Now, you'll pay out through my account in Grand Cayman, is that correct? Good. . . . Of course Freddy knows all about . . . right. An orderly exit. Exactly. That's every-thing is it? . . . My pleasure. Bye-bye. (*hangs up*)

JILL

It's done?

CLARE

Apparently. Feel better?

JILL

Glad to be out of it, but not better. Glad Peter's out of it. You really shouldn't have brought him into it.

CLARE

I merely pointed out the benefits for his career.

JILL

Between what I did, and you, and Freddy-bloody-Boise, I think he feels quite soiled.

CLARE

On the contrary, all I see are his sterling qualities. His understanding, his loyalty. He didn't have to warn me about Life Products.

As CLARE talks, PETER appears dressed in David Ashe's period costume. He bows to JILL and JILL sees that he has no arms. She puts the infant on the settee and takes PETER by his jacket sleeves and begins to dance with him.

JILL

(*dancing*) Please don't—

CLARE

It's been my experience that while we may occasionally be seduced by personality, what we really love is character. Peter has character. Your father had character.

JILL

(*dancing*) But you two weren't happy

CLARE

We had a very good, very stable life together. However much I might have disparaged him, I never lost my respect for him. I made the right choice.

KILMAN enters wearing David Ashe's wig and mask, and cuts in on the dance.

JILL

I can't believe that if I was living the right life, I can't believe I wouldn't be happy.

CLARE

Are you really so unhappy with Peter?

JILL

I wish it was that simple.

CLARE

I almost made the same mistake. Almost cancelled the wedding.

JILL

Never.

The light flares upon BOISE in his office. He puts out his arms to dance. JILL backs away.

CLARE

There was a fellow . . . he had a crude but overpowering personality. . . . Actually, he frightened me, and for a time I thought that fear was love.

JILL

Freddy Boise.

JILL, while staring at BOISE, picks up a remote-control switch which manages to both turn off the music and make BOISE, PETER, and KILMAN disappear.

CLARE

We should put you on a game show.

JILL

(*sitting down*) Did Dad know about—?

CLARE

They weren't actually at the same time. Freddy had gone off to Europe on some stock scheme and then I met your father, who was on the rebound from Kathleen.

JILL

Kathleen? Kate Riley?

CLARE

(*pouring tea with a strainer*) He told you?

JILL

But she drowned in the pond.

CLARE

What pond?

JILL

At Burnham Wood. When she was ten.

CLARE

Impossible.

JILL

I remember because Dad told me when we planted my tenth birthday tree.

CLARE

Well, she was still very much alive a year before our wedding.

JILL

But why would he lie if she didn't?

CLARE

It's a far more romantic ending, but I'm afraid the truth is rather pedestrian. Kathleen was a lot older than David and she was married. Back then, that qualified as a scandal.

JILL

What happened?

CLARE

Grandma Ashe put a stop to it.

JILL

Did she threaten to disinherit him?

CLARE

Might have done.

JILL

Maybe there's a connection between Dad giving up Kate and then finally giving up his inheritance.

CLARE

Thirty-three years after the fact? Hardly.

JILL

She was pregnant.

CLARE

Please. It wasn't a nineteenth-century novel. At best, it was a brief encounter. Grandma told Kathleen's husband and they disappeared. The end. Moved to Rhodesia, I think. Anyway, she certainly didn't drown. They moved on, and David and I started going together. (*pause*) Jilly . . . I realize that . . . well . . . a lot goes unsaid between us . . . and I'm content to fill in the empty spaces if that's all you want . . . but I don't think that's why you came.

The phone rings as the light comes up on BOISE's space. He's on the phone.

JILL

You know how you always say I do things by half—

CLARE

I don't *really* mean—

JILL

This time, I'm afraid I've done it all the way.

CLARE puts up her hand as if to say "hold that thought" and picks up the phone.

BOISE

(*ranting*) You want the other arm!

CLARE

Hello, Freddy.

BOISE

I do one decent thing in my life, I let you into my deal, a deal I created out of nothing, a year of my goddamn life, and just when it's going through the roof—you blow me off.

CLARE

(*calmly*) Freddy.

BOISE

Life Products is set to make a new offer—seventy goddamn nine.

CLARE

I'm happy for you.

BOISE

You know what the stock is doing? It's running down my leg, Clare. It's a fucking puddle because you and Peter blew me off without so much as a word.

CLARE

Always such a gentleman.

BOISE

The fucking public aren't going to hear about that offer, Clare, because you and the little Polack have handed the company to the Japs. By the end of the day, they'll be over the top, they'll get control.

CLARE

I suggest you get some too, Freddy. There's no sense talking about meals we haven't eaten. Just get up from the table and sell.

BOISE

We could have had eighty.

CLARE

It's only business. Now, when you calm down I'll make you dinner.

JILL begins breast-feeding the infant.

BOISE

Dinner?

CLARE

Food, Freddy. The reason you started working. Remember?

BOISE

(*affectionately*) You're the damnedest.

CLARE

Say, Saturday, seven-thirty?

BOISE

(*smiling*) You think you know just what I want, don't you?

CLARE

Need. What you need, Freddy. Jill's here. Got to go. Bye.

CLARE hangs up and BOISE goes to black.

JILL

He's upset?

CLARE

(*smiling*) Freddy is his old self once again.

JILL

You still like him?

CLARE

I used to be afraid of him, but now he amuses me because he's so obvious.

JILL

Kind of boorish, isn't he?

CLARE

Yes, but if it were not for pigs digging in the dirt, we wouldn't have truffles.

JILL

What happened to character?

CLARE

I'm only your mother, Jill. I'm not a role model. (*beat*) Now, you have dropped this water fellow, haven't you?

JILL

I'm not certain I want to, now.

CLARE

But you love Peter?

JILL

You loved Dad, didn't you?

CLARE

Could we keep this conversation in the present tense? Whether I—

JILL

I'm pregnant.

CLARE

Pardon?

JILL

I haven't seen a doctor, or done any tests, but I know.

CLARE

Would you please get a test? Before you—

JILL

I know.

CLARE

Your father didn't put you through university for you to use your intuition. And I suppose it's quite possibly his?

JILL nods yes.

And you won't consider. . . .

JILL

I've already had two.

CLARE

Hillary said one.

JILL

Two.

CLARE

Well, it seems you've decided. Not sure what to say. You have your own money now and . . . I wish you'd stopped me from rambling on about Peter. I . . . what to say? I suppose we'd better meet him.

JILL

(*calls out*) Paul!

KILMAN appears as the lights shift to a starry night at the woods.

CLARE

If that's his name. You could bring him to dinner on Saturday and . . . would you please see a doctor?

JILL nods and hands CLARE the baby.

And I won't be called Grandma . . . and . . . God, Jilly, this time you've really silenced me.

CLARE exits.

SCENE 17

KILMAN and JILL at the pond.

JILL

The other day I phoned the lawn people, to invite you, and they said you don't work there—never have.

KILMAN

Sometimes the facts don't tell you anything.

JILL

Please, it's so much bullshit.

KILMAN

I'm not what you're looking for. I'm not. I'd like to be, want to be, but I'm not. At least I can't be out there.

JILL

Hold me.

KILMAN

You hold something in the dark and you can imagine it's anything—

JILL

An oak—

KILMAN

Anyone. But anything pure is a fragile thing. Someone always turns on the lights. This isn't something we could sustain.

JILL

You make breaking up feel romantic.

KILMAN

How do I say it? I'm trying to be objective about this.

JILL

Don't. Let's not talk about what is, or is not, objectively, the case. Maybe I imagined you were someone else. Maybe I though I was. I could raise my voice and call you a liar.

KILMAN

Do it. Call me a liar.

JILL

The truth is, I've used you. Not only you, but Peter, my father, this place. It's as if I've been trying to graft on some missing part. And I have this horrible feeling that if I don't find it, I'll keep fucking up other people's lives.

KILMAN

It could be the other way round. It could be other people who are screwing up yours.

JILL

Don't believe in conspiracy theories.

KILMAN

Anyway, you haven't screwed up my life. If anything you've unscrewed it.

JILL

Things usually fall apart if they get unscrewed.

KILMAN

I've kept all the pieces.

JILL

And you'll remember where they go?

KILMAN

The heart goes in the middle somewhere.

JILL

(*kisses him*) I'll miss you, Paul. Paul, is that really your name?

The lights come up on the crocodile, which has BOISE's arm coming out of its mouth.

KILMAN

Whatever happens, Jill, I want you to understand, this is who I was.

JILL

(*staring at the crocodile*) Why say that?

KILMAN

I just don't want you to think of me like the girl who was supposed to be in the pond. What happened between us, it did really happen—didn't it?

KILMAN walks over to BOISE's office. JILL lies on the bed.

SCENE 18

KILMAN is going through BOISE's desk as DEE enters. PETER comes down to the pond carrying a bottle of champagne.

DEE

You wanted to see me?

KILMAN

The petty cash cheques—

DEE

Uh—well . . . I can explain. I . . . I—

KILMAN

Two a week over the last ten months. I've got your bank statements. Using your personal account, very sloppy.

PETER

Jill!

DEE

What are you going to do about it?

KILMAN

You know how to access Boise's private trading accounts.

DEE

That's Angel's job. I don't—

KILMAN

You've stolen over a quarter of a million. Do I pick up the phone?

DEE

All I know is, Angel buys stock on the Tokyo exchange through a bank in Hong Kong.

KILMAN

And the profit—

DEE

It goes through Switzerland and then it's transferred to Panama.

Not finding JILL, PETER decides to leave the champagne. He goes to exit, then turns back and taps the bottle into the pond with his foot. Exits.

KILMAN

Access the codes, Dee.

DEE

(*frightened*) He . . . he doesn't trust me that much and the important stuff is on a microchip in his arm. It is—

KILMAN

How did we get so ugly?

DEE

Sir?

KILMAN

You get on the elevator, hardly feels like you're moving, but you're going down. Down, and it's like you're not thinking, or you're looking at your watch and you miss the lobby, and end up in the fucking furnace ! Push the goddamn buttons! (*smashes his hand on the desk*) Now!

DEE quickly pushes some buttons on the terminal embedded in the desk. We hear the sound of a printer.

BLACKOUT.

SCENE 19

This scene between KILMAN and BOISE takes place in BOISE's office. It could be staged that way, but it should be done on video, either live offstage or on tape. If on video, the blacks fly up to reveal a large office tower with a city panorama in the background. The tower contains many lit offices, and implanted in the top floor are several small video monitors. The scene is captured as if we were watching the windows of BOISE's office from a rooftop across the street, so we would see BOISE and KILMAN move about the office appearing in one monitor, then another—which is precisely what the authorities are now seeing. We hear the conversation with perhaps some distortion through loudspeakers.

KILMAN

(*seeing BOISE enter*) I found the man you were looking for.

BOISE

And—

KILMAN

At first I thought I was the one who was sucking her in.

BOISE

You? You're the guy?

KILMAN

She was telling me about black holes, how they suck everything in. I thought I was growing, expanding. Kilman's my bright light, you said. Kilman's a smart little shit, you said. Kilman knows what Lee Iacocca had for breakfast.

BOISE

It's what you've been eating that concerns me. I'm

disappointed in you, Kilman. (*approaches his desk*) I thought we were a team. I trusted you to—(*picks up one paper, then another*) How did you get—what the fuck is this?

KILMAN

(*enjoying himself*) They're copies. You should have seen the guys at the Securities Commission when I walked in. Accountants who hadn't left their chairs in twenty years got up and danced. Ever seen an accountant dance, Freddy?

BOISE

You son-of-a-bitch, you didn't?

KILMAN

I did. And not just the Life Products takeover. All the way back, Freddy. Nine years. Any idea of how many board meetings I've wired for you?

BOISE

And did I ever hear those tapes? It's your word against mine.

KILMAN

They've got every transaction for the last nine years.

BOISE

(*holding up the documents*) You think you can mess with me? Switzerland, Panama—you've pulled two knots out of a Persian rug.

KILMAN

They know about Hong Kong, about Angel—

BOISE

Angel lives on an island in the south Pacific. They'll

never deport him, and even if he showed up dancing on the head of a pin, the only thing he knows is that there's a God and his name is Freddy Boise. You think you know something, then tell me who owns Life Products. The Japs? You don't know sushi. *They* don't even know that *I* fucking own them, so don't go pulling on my fly. (*pause*) Why? Goddamn it! You were a partner. You were like a son.

KILMAN

(*laughing*) I was the daughter you never had.

BOISE

You should have come to me if there was something serious between you and Jill. We could have come up with some story.

KILMAN

But not the truth!

BOISE

We're talking about a woman here!

KILMAN

And what truth could I tell her? The half truth? The whole truth? The truth about you? About me? I see it all spinning around, the truth chasing the lies. It's my whole life! It's like pissing into a whirlpool.

BOISE

You know what you're doing here? Bottom line, I can buy my way out. But even if you co-operate, it's a sentence, Kilman. Prison. Are you listening? Prison. Two years, Kilman! Look at me!

KILMAN

Every time you make a deal you say it's better than

pissing on your boots. It isn't. They're going to close us down, Freddy. They're going to put the lid down and flush.

BOISE

Some interesting circumstantial evidence, but it all comes down to your word against mine and—

KILMAN

(*waves out the window*) They've got yours on tape. See that man across the way?

BOISE

Where? Where? I don't see anything. I don't see—(*pause*) Christ.

SCENE 20

PETER *is having tea with* CLARE. JILL *is studying something down by the pond.*

CLARE

(*stirs the tea in the pot*) It meant giving up your fund, didn't it? (*puts the lid back on*)

PETER

By the time the Securities Commission finishes their investigation, I doubt I'll have a fund.

CLARE

Freddy said they'll never prove you knew what would happen.

PETER

True. But as an ecological fund I promised my investors not to buy certain stocks.

CLARE

(*pouring tea with a strainer*) Like Life Products?

PETER

(*nods yes*) Anyway, taking the job at Sirroco Energy allows me a . . . graceful out. And since the employees own thirty per cent of the stock, it's not a very attractive candidate for takeover. (*about to add milk to his tea, CLARE takes it*)

CLARE

Have you talked to Jill? That's cream.

PETER

I'd like to . . .

CLARE rings a small bell.

. . . but we agreed not to see each other for two months. Actually, I went up last week, but she wasn't there.

CLARE

(*rings bell again*) I'm afraid it's all too modern for me. Where's Magdelaina?

BOISE enters with a newspaper, wearing a hook instead of his artificial arm.

CLARE

You're just in time for tea.

BOISE

Look at this. Kilman gets a colour picture, I get a black and white. (*throws the paper down*)

JILL picks up the paper BOISE threw down and starts reading.

CLARE

(*noticing the hook*) Where's your arm?

BOISE

It's been subpoenaed.

PETER

Your arm?

BOISE

Yes.

CLARE

Am I to understand that your arm has been taken in for questioning?

BOISE

It knows a lot about the business.

CLARE

Your arm?

BOISE

Yes!

CLARE

(*after a beat*) Do you mean it talks?

BOISE

It contains some account numbers.

PETER

(*laughing*) I wonder if they'll give it immunity?

BOISE

One word from me and it'll finger you.
Pause.

CLARE

Peter's just been telling me about his new job.

PETER

President of Sirroco Energy.

BOISE

(*smiling*) They called me for a reference.

PETER

They what?

BOISE

I had to convince them you were ruthless enough.

PETER

Don't tell me this.

BOISE

I've looked at their numbers. It's a good opportunity. A company poised for expansion. I could help.

CLARE

Frederick, you are not allowed to trade—

BOISE

A hundred and twenty-eight million, that's what I'm offering to settle. They'll let me keep playing.

CLARE

(*to BOISE*) Find a hobby. I'm sorry, Peter, I'll get some milk.

BOISE

(*to CLARE*) So it's not my name out front. I could still—

CLARE exits with the cream.

PETER

Freddy, it would be so easy to let you in the back door, and the terrible thing is . . . I want to. That's why I won't.

BOISE

I don't follow.

PETER

Because a part of me likes you. I could be like you.

BOISE

A success.

PETER

Have the world laid out before me in a straight line. Everything certain, and money the answer to every question. (*whispering so CLARE won't hear*) God, to have the luxury of your contempt. Buy 'em—sell 'em—fuck 'em! The easiness of it, to be so fashionably stupid and indifferent to anything but my own power!

BOISE

Admit it, Peter. It's your fantasy.

PETER

It's a nightmare.

The lights flare up on David Ashe, his head emerging from the pond. He raises his hand up as if to strike JILL. It is a large hook. She recoils, then regains herself, calls out in realization, "Dad. Daddy." David Ashe submerges and as he does we realize that he is half man, half crocodile. His tail splashes the water and then he is gone. JILL runs off with the newspaper.

CLARE

Milk. . . . Did you tell him?

BOISE

Should I? (*CLARE smiles*) Do you know who stood by me these last weeks? Days I usually get two hundred calls, only one person called.

PETER

Clare?

BOISE

We're getting married. (*goes to pour milk in his tea*)

PETER

To each other?

CLARE

(*intercepting BOISE's milk*) You're having lemon.

BOISE

Am I?

CLARE nods.

PETER

(*surprised*) You two, married?

CLARE

Someone has to take care of this wounded animal.

PETER laughs.

BOISE

What's so funny, I couldn't be a husband?

PETER

No. I'm thinking of Jill.

JILL enters, heading to BOISE's office.

She can't get you out of her dreams, and now she won't be able to get you out of her life.

BOISE

I'll be her father.

CLARE

Her *step*father.

SCENE 21

JILL is walking slowly as she enters BOISE's office while reading the newspaper. DEE is packing up her things.

JILL

He wanted to tell me. I know he did. He said, whatever happens—

DEE

He said what was most profitable to him—at the moment. You're hurt, angry, feel like you've been raped. One, two, three, now do something.

JILL

He refused bail. I went to the prison. Wouldn't see me.

DEE

C'mon, Kilman knows all about shorting stock. He's thinking, how can I profit from this? That's what men do. You're just a situation to him, and he'll slice and dice you until you're the one begging him for forgiveness.

JILL

Things can't be that ugly.

DEE

Profit and loss, the weak and the strong. It's not complex, Jill. The key to survival is to adopt a strategy which turns your weakness into strength.

JILL

I should get going.

DEE

What am I, some bimbo? I don't know from Darwin?

JILL

No, I—I came to see Boise.

DEE

Good. You're thinking "Freddy." What's the strategy?

JILL

I don't have any—

DEE

First, you've got to take all these random events and order them to your advantage. Boise and your mother, the hiring of Peter—the Kilman factor, this tape—

JILL

What's that?

DEE

Peter moving into your place. I thought Boise was checking up on Peter, but the courts won't—

JILL

Courts?

DEE

Step two, the slice and dice. You can make a killing suing Boise. Invasion of privacy, paternity, emotional damages—work the angles, that's how you turn weaknesses into strength. You take the stand, the cameras, the tabloids, the tears running down your face. You're a natural.

JILL

You're a man, right? You're a man dressed in drag, right?

The lights come up on CLARE and FREDDY. JILL's bed has become CLARE's.

DEE

I'm a survivor. (*points to her hair, pulls off her wig*) Despair won't change anything. It takes strategy. I sit down, cross my legs, put my tits on the table (*takes out falsies*), and guys go blind. They don't think straight 'cause the blood isn't going to their head. See, I hold out the promise of conquest. Guy who thinks you're stupid and attainable throws caution to the wind. And that's when I go for the cheque-book.

As she talks, DEE reveals herself to be nothing at all as we imagined. Even her true voice is different.

JILL

You sell yourself to—

DEE

No, I don't have sex—with anyone. I'm against it.

JILL

What—you steal from them.

DEE

I could finance the court case.

JILL

You stole from Boise?

DEE

It's not stealing, it's guerrilla warfare. You know about

imperialism? Whites penetrating darkest Africa? That's sex, Jill. Penetration is imperialism plain and simple. (*she puts the tape of JILL and PETER into a hidden video machine and plays the tape*) The way I see it, it's the responsibility of women to refuse to have sex until men start seeing hidden beauty. When guys start fantasizing about Mother Teresa, then we can talk. (*swivels around in BOISE's chair*)

SCENE 22

CLARE's bedroom. JILL and CLARE are arguing. BOISE in his housecoat stands near the bed.

CLARE

You come in here accusing Freddy, attacking me and my character in the name of truth! The truth—what difference? You had a father who loved you. (*clicks off the video playing in BOISE's office with a remote control*)

JILL

I had a right to—

CLARE

You get a positive thrill out of your rights, especially when you know others will be hurt. That's not morality, young lady, it's sheer malevolence.

BOISE

We were going to tell you.

CLARE

(*to BOISE*) We were not! Until your damn scientists, no one knew for certain, only me. Everyone believed she was David's child, and so did he.

JILL

You never let him make that choice.

CLARE

It was a minor detail.

JILL

Maybe that's how it started, but every time you saw him take my hand, every time you heard him introduce me, added to it. And it kept multiplying until you had no room for anything but your own guilt.

CLARE

(*rapidly*) Do you imagine I spent the last thirty-two years of my life feeling guilty because you were born into a good home and a life of privilege? Because you had parents who loved you? Or guilty because I fucked—yes, I do know the verb—I fucked Freddy Boise and had a good time of it? I'm not going to allow you to come in here looking for melodrama. We were a happy family, we are a happy family, and it's going to stay a happy family!

BOISE

You're damn right we're a family! And that means this home should be the one place, the one bloody sanctuary where all is forgiven, where every handicap and inadequacy is finally understood! (*takes off his false arm and puts it on the night table*)

JILL

And what am I to understand? That it's all right for you to crawl into my life like some reptile? At least we won't have to waste time catching up, now that Kilman's told you all the intimate details.

BOISE

He's the enemy. He's the one who caused this.

JILL

Thanks for clearing that up, Dad. I should have understood that it's all right for you to deceive and manipulate everyone because basically you're loving parents.

CLARE

If you can't keep a civil tongue—

JILL

I'm tired of being polite and I'm tired of the indifference to my concerns.

BOISE

Indifference! I'm facing criminal charges because I tried to help you. We dirtied our hands to protect—(*goes to his desk and takes out the mortgage*) This is all you care about. A thousand bloody acres. (*throws JILL the mortgage*) Go on. Take it, it's all yours. And as far as I'm concerned, you can go up there and lock the gate.

JILL

You're right. What good is anything wild? We're civilized people here. We're grown up, and I've got to realize that everything I love, everything I believe in, that little bit of nature—it's unnatural! Isn't that right, Dad? I've got to stop listening to my heart and face the facts. I should put down all these pet emotions. It's more sanitary to have them stuffed and displayed like all the other arte-facts which go so well with our décor. Why bother to empathize, when I can possess?

BOISE

What the hell is she on about?

JILL

I'm sorry to be such a bad investment. I know I should be reasonable and realize just how much we have. On the one hand we have our power and on the other—(*picks up his arm on the night table*) There is no other hand! We cut it off because it was asking too many questions. We chopped it off and don't feel it anymore. (*bangs the hand on the bed*) We don't feel anything (*the hand starts to move its fingers*), but the hand goes on, connected to no-one. It goes on and on and on . . . but how can I? What place is left for me? Why did you give me values if there isn't a world to put them in?

CLARE

(*softly*) I . . . you were my secret, don't you understand? For once I had something that was just mine. The clothes on my back, the thoughts in my head, they belonged to other people. But not you. You were my secret. No one knew the truth, and by God I wasn't going to give it to them. Because it made me strong, you see. You were my only protection, and as long as I had you I never had to surrender. I knew you thought I was cold, but I always held you in my heart. I just needed you, Jilly, just this one thing that made me, me.

After a beat, JILL breaks away from CLARE and runs out. CLARE calls after her, "Jilly." She runs out. BLACKOUT. Howling winds blow as lights up on snow falling.

Time passes. PETER and HILLARY enter. CLARE's space now suggests HILLARY's apartment. PETER throws his coat on the settee. The next scene has begun.

SCENE 23

At home HILLARY seems quite childlike. She wears pink sweats and too-cute slippers. The final three scenes play as one.

HILLARY

Would you stop? She's not dead. She's probably on a beach somewhere. (*handing PETER a drink*)

PETER

It's been six months.

HILLARY

She's just being dramatic. Remember that scene in the theatre? She got better reviews than the play.

PETER

You think so?

HILLARY

Yes. I'm not saying she'll be back—but do you really want her back? Do you want to spend your life like this? It won't end. You know that don't you? There'll be another crisis.

PETER

I want her to be okay. I haven't thought about me.

HILLARY

Well, I have. I've been trying to be of some comfort, but I'd be lying if I didn't tell you I was tired of holding the door for Jillson. I've grown very fond of you, Peter.

PETER laughs awkwardly.

I have. You're bright, attractive—

PETER

Ethnic—

HILLARY

Ethnics are very hip right now.

PETER

So is that what you're into? What happened to your junior partner?

HILLARY

That was fiction. It kept Mom off my back. And me on it.

PETER

You know the problem with living?

HILLARY

The hours.

PETER

It's people like you who use the rest of us to set up your punch lines.

HILLARY

Peter, we're alive. Babies, fish, the guy picking his nose at the light, they're funny. Only the dead are serious. Or maybe you have to be there to get their jokes.

PETER

I have to go.

HILLARY

Peter. I care about you. C'mon, stop whipping yourself.

PETER

I have to see this through.

HILLARY

Listen. When I was a kid, Mum used to call Dad a romantic. I didn't know what it meant, so I asked him, and he said it's "someone who thinks that today is yesterday." But that's not romance, it's pessimism.

PETER

I used to know what I wanted. But now I can't work, can't make love, not that there's—

HILLARY

Stay. (*kisses him*)

PETER

It's almost tempting.

HILLARY

Stay. (*kiss*) One more drink. (*long kiss*) She's not dead.

PETER

(*as he exits to the pond*) No—we are.

He picks up his briefcase and as he turns, a policewoman enters from upstage and CLARE from the wings. HILLARY lies on the settee.

SCENE 24

PETER and CLARE at the pond. A policewoman in shiny shades is also present. She is examining an algae-covered female pelvic bone.

COP

When did you say she disappeared?

CLARE

(*wiping away the tears*) About six months ago.

PETER

(*comforting CLARE*) It can't be her.

COP

I'm no pathologist, but I'd say this has been in there a long time.

PETER

How long?

COP

Who knows? Could be thirty, forty years.

CLARE

Kate. It has to be Kate.

PETER

Who's—

CLARE

Kathleen Riley. My husband—my first husband—once told my daughter that Kate drowned here. I didn't believe it, I—thank God, it's not—

COP

When was this—

CLARE

If it's true, it would be . . . thirty-five years ago.

COP

And he didn't report it?

A diver wearing a scuba tank emerges from the pond. We just see the back of his head. He hands the cop another bone.

DIVER

There's a great trench down the middle, foot wide, and Christ knows how deep. She's wedged in.

COP

Keep at it, Jimmy. I'll radio forensics.

166

166

DIVER

Tell 'em to bring their rods. There's great trout. (*submerges*)

COP

If you'll excuse me, Mrs. Boise. (*exits*)

We hear the sound of a chainsaw coming from behind the audience.

PETER

She's not down there, Clare.

CLARE

I wanted to—I had to do something. She's taking nothing from her account—gone without a trace—I can't. . . . Look at poor Freddy over there. (*pointing at the audience*) Won't say a word. He just keeps cutting down trees. Won't acknowledge it. Maybe he blames himself, maybe he doesn't care. I don't know what he's feeling.

PETER

And you? Are you two really going to move up here?

CLARE

(*nods no*) I just wanted to fix up the house—in case she wants it—if she ever. . . . (*pause*) There's a stream down there. It leads—I don't know where it leads. She used to hide down there, thought I didn't know about it. Walk with me, Peter. I'm afraid in the woods.

They exit off.

SCENE 25

BOISE immediately enters, perhaps through the audience. He's dressed for the country and carries a chainsaw. He coughs occasionally. As he walks past the pond, a drowning hand reaches out from the water in desperation. BOISE drops the chainsaw and grabs the hand. A naked JILL emerges, her back to us. She walks up the hill and disappears.

BOISE

(*as JILL heads out*) Jill? Jilly. . . . Clare! (*to himself*) She was . . . (*keeps looking at the pond, then up the hill, quietly*) Jill. . . .

CLARE and PETER enter.

CLARE

We were just heading down to the. . . What's happened? (*rushes to him*) Freddy?

BOISE

(*slowly, after a beat*) She held my hand. I helped her out, you see . . . and she held my hand. . . .

CLARE looks to PETER, then back to BOISE.

CLARE

(*tenderly*) Come on, let's go back to the house. There's tea. (*she goes to lead BOISE out, but they don't exit*)

The diver re-emerges from the pond and puts a skull and PETER's bottle of champagne down. PETER turns in time to see him re-submerge.

PETER

(*picking up the chainsaw*) I'll make a fire.

SCENE 26

As JILL walks down the hill, the light and sound indicate we're in Africa.

JILL

How do we reconcile the fact of evolution, the

creation of highly ordered species, with the second
law of thermodynamics, which tells us that disorder
is constantly increasing? (*indicating student*) Hold on,
Manu.

Most of us would have to concede that the evolution
of reason, of technology, and the logic of democracy are
just a few things which have brought a greater order to the
world around us. But if that's the case, why is it that *inside*
so many of us increasingly feel like prisoners of our own
chaos? Unable to protest, unable to reach out, invisible in
this, the best of all possible worlds? Munyama? (*indicating
student*) Well, I'm glad you don't—maybe it's just me?
When I first came to Zimbabwe with my daughter I
suppose I naively hoped to create a new world, for us.
But there really only is one world, isn't there? Chinuea,
it was a rhetorical question.

Now, when I imagine all those I left behind, those
whose values seemed so contrary to my own, it occurs
to me that through their greed and deceit, they, like me,
have withdrawn from the world.

*DEE appears at BOISE's desk and KILMAN can be seen in CLARE's
foyer.*

Whether in luxury or poverty it seems we've all withdrawn into our own personal chaos.

A slide of the earth taken from space is projected in the distance.

Apparently there's a highly evolved, highly ordered world
out there, but who's living in it? Manu? . . . Yes, I know
I've gone off the topic—again. What is this obsession of
yours for staying on topic? We'll never learn anything
about the spot we're standing on, unless we walk around it.
And please, stop calling me "Miss Riley." It's "Kate.". . .
Now, where *are* we?

Bang out the lights.

*Curtain call. Chase the audience out with something aggressive like
Lou Reed's "There Is No Time" from the album* New York.

End

AFTERWORD

Quantum mechanics, real estate, environmentalism, feminism, consumerism, Peter Pan, and the stock market. And that's not *The Half of It*. John Krizanc's latest play is a complex, witty exploration of the nature and implications of the dominant world view that underlies humanism, evolutionary theory, the scientific method, contemporary Christianity, capitalism, and Cartesian logic, the world view that has shaped Western society since the Renaissance.

It is not surprising that John Krizanc should write a sophisticated play that reflects contemporary intellectual activity in human terms. What is surprising is that this most cerebral of Canadian playwrights should insist so strongly on the need for a balance between linear thought and instinct, feeling, mysticism, and randomness; or that a playwright known for his critiques of political extremism should portray so acutely in the character of Peter the futility and naïveté of the liberal "middle ground" in the face of powerful self-interest. Peter's world of "environmentally friendly" products and investments is, finally, no different from the ruthless, greedy speculator Boise's world, where "idealism has to surrender to practicality" because "people change in direct proportion to their self-interest." Once this "practical," "common sense" approach to social change *within* the dominant world view is adopted, fundamental change that derives rom changes in the way we think and see is presented as being impossible. "Goodness" becomes merely something that, as Boise says, "there's money in," and "the key to survival"—defined by his secretary, Dee, in explicitly Darwinian terms—"is to adopt a strategy which turns your weakness into strength."

The challenge for Krizanc in writing a play about these issues was to find a form that would reflect and reinforce his concerns rather than subvert or assimilate them by employing traditionally linear dramaturgical devices that themselves embody the dominant world view. Krizanc is best known, of course, for his environmental-theatre, antifascist masterpiece, *Tamara*, which uses simultaneous staging in various rooms of a house to give choices back to the audience, thereby deconstructing what Krizanc sees as the fascism of the theatre itself.

The Half of It is related to *Tamara* and to Krizanc's Governor General's award-winning play *Prague* in both form and subject matter. *The Half of It* extends the earlier plays' exploration of the contemporary liberal stance, and like them uses an innovative, metatheatrical form that reflects and reinforces the play's themes. Largely about perception, about ways of seeing, ordering, and understanding the world, *The Half of It* consistently disrupts our expectations as comfortably distanced spectators and forces us to see and understand differently. Through the use of actors as audiences, simultaneous staging, flexible barriers between conventionally discrete playing spaces, video monitors, walk-through walls, ghosts, crocodiles, drowning girls, alter-egos, and characters who overhear and spy on other characters, Krizanc forges a form that replaces traditional logocentric theatrical structures with ones that are more flexible, open, and more appropriate to his subject.

As in *Prague*, and appropriately in a play that attempts to do for theatre what quantum physics has done for science, the characters in *The Half of It* are spectators and actors at once. There is in the play's form as well as its content a sense of parallel universe, of multiple perspectives. As *Tamara* and *Prague* explode the tyranny of traditional theatrical wisdom about unifying directorial concepts and theatrical focus, *The Half of It* attempts a new dramaturgy that resists what the playwright calls "Newtonian" concepts such as the "trajectory of a character," together with the traditional through-lines, rising actions, climaxes, and turning points of dramatic action.

Krizanc says that he has tried to learn from quantum physics in his construction of character and plot, and he talks of Jillson Ashe as a "quantum character." She is often the spokesperson for the play's central concerns, as in the wonderful opening monologue, yet she is not an entirely sympathetic or dramatically consistent character. The audience is not allowed simply to adopt her perspective or see the world of the play through her eyes, nor are her choices endorsed by the play. Krizanc sees reflected in her withdrawal from responsible action that of his own generation of intellectuals and artists, himself included. Their passivity, he feels, makes them "guilty of all the things that they have contempt for." Boise recognizes this condition when he asks Peter, "Why do you think they're always putting up statues to people with integrity? Because they're monuments to inaction." And as Jill's sister, Hillary, tells her, "People are interested in what you do—*do*—in the world. . . . Feeling is *not* an event, it is *not* an accomplishment, and it is not something people want to know. Good night." The play ends with Jill's realization that her withdrawal is in effect no different from Peter's collaboration or Boise's greed. She is finally and ironically her father's daughter.

If Krizanc's characters are as multidimensional and inconsistent as most people, so his plot resists the linear development of cause and effect, together with the resolution of either/or dichotomies in a central action. An audience at a performance of *The Half of It* will experience neither the satisfying, ultimately passive experience of cathartic release nor the curiously fashionable thrill of futile self-flagellation. Rather, it will be forced actively to construct its own position in relation to the play world and shape for itself the play's meaning. The audience is complicit in the play in the same way the scientist is complicit in his or her experiment: even as the act of observing electrons in motion affects that motion, the act of watching the play affects the play's meaning. In a world without wholly objective truths, meaning depends upon the viewer.

As the play's most perceptive if also most successfully self-interested character, Dee, puts it, "You've got to take all these random events and order them to your own advantage."

The Half of It is not, of course, without its own clutch of viewpoints, but those viewpoints do not consist of reductive choices between the opposing poles of such Cartesian dichotomies posed by the play as mind vs body, active vs contemplative, objective vs subjective, reason vs emotion, civilization vs nature, urban vs rural or male vs female—dichotomies that inevitably privilege the former term. For Krizanc, to view the world as presenting a series of unacceptable alternatives leads to withdrawal or co-option, and choosing between such alternatives leads to the willful subjection of nature, women or whatever "the other half" may be. In *The Half of It* John Krizanc is trying to find a way to see differently, to take responsibility for what and how we see, and to turn dichotomies into dualities. He wants to achieve a balanced coexistence within the individual, in society, and in nature. As he puts it, he wants to find a way, in art and in the world, to embrace and celebrate "the other half of the other half of it."

RICHARD PAUL KNOWLES
Department of Drama
University of Guelph